PUERTO RICO TRUE·FLAVORS
BY WILO BENET

MRG - San Juan, Puerto Rico

Read Street Publishing Inc · Tropical Dining Press
Baltimore, Maryland

Puerto Rico
True Flavors
by Wilo Benet

ISBN: 978-0-942929-26-3
LCCN: 2006938190
(Library of Congress Preassigned Control Number)

© Wilo Benet 2007
All rights reserved
No part of this book may be reproduced or utilized
in any form or by any means, electronic or mechanical,
including photocopying, recording, or by any information
storage or retrieval system, without the written permission
of the copyright holder.

Pikayo and Payá Restaurants
Museum Restaurant Group
P.O. Box 16619
San Juan, PR 00918
Tel. 787-751-1124
Fax. 787-751-7054

www.wilobenet.com
info@wilobenet.com

recipe editor: Viviana Acosta Padial
photographer: Jose Soto
graphic design: Viviré - Creative & Interactive Studio

book editor: Barbara Tasch Ezratty

Published by Tropical Dining Press
A division of Read Street Publishing Inc.
133 W. Read Street
Baltimore, MD 21201
1-888-964-BOOK

Printed in China

To Lorraine, Gonzalo & Lucas

For all the days and nights I know they would rather have shared with me but, patiently and understandingly, continued with their lives without me at home while I labored with my professional mission, wishing I was there with them.

With all my love.

Acknowledgements

In a career spanning almost 25 years - so far - it is hard to mention everyone who has contributed to the development of my achievements, but I promise to do my very best.

First and foremost, I have to start by thanking my grandparents, Manolín, Milagros, William & Evelyn, who greatly contributed to my education; to my parents Willie & Milagros, who laid everything on the line to support my first restaurant, now 17 years old, and showed me the value of honesty, hard work, attention to detail and the importance of treating others the same way I would want to be treated; to my in-laws Maruja and Ito, as well as my sister-in-law Ambar, who cared for Gonzalo & Lucas; and to my companion in life, Lorraine, my wife of 18 years, tireless partner and source of inspiration in many ways.

Thanks also to *Tío* Quique and Rosi for giving me shelter and protecting me when my actions were ahead of my better judgment.

Thanks to my dear friend and second father figure Carlos Matos who, without really knowing me that well back then, contributed to my cause. To Manuel & Ninette Méndez, who also supported me in the very beginning.

To Augusto Shreiner, who gave me my very first real opportunity in a kitchen at the Caribe Hilton Hotel in San Juan, where I acted as apprentice under the supervision of Augusto himself as well as Joseph Stevenson, Norbert Bomm, Willie Nunlist, Pancho and Rafi Pambuan.

To the Honorable Rafael Hernández Colón, Governor of Puerto Rico, who gave me an opportunity to serve Puerto Rico from the kitchens of the Governor's Mansion. And to all the Puerto Ricans and people of the world who through the years sponsored my restaurants with their visits.

To Ivette Sepúlveda, who provided the final push for me to get started with this project.

To the staffs of Pikayo, Payá, MRG & MCS who so intensely work day in and day out, pouring their hearts and efforts into our products and services.

Thanks to the banking institutions in Puerto Rico that have had the confidence to back the continued development of my restaurants and catering business: Without their help, I wouldn't be where I am today.

I would also like to thank Barbara Tasch Ezratty, José Soto, Viviana Acosta Padial, María Elena Pérez, Edgardo Jiménez, George Schminky, Iko Negrón and Jorge Marchand for their commitment and efforts in this project.

Special thanks to Carli and Jorge Unanue of Goya.

Finally, to God who has stuck with me through thick and thin, providing the talents, blessings and opportunities present in my life.

Wilo Benet

Contents

Section I. Basics:
- 5 Introduction
- 6 *Aceite de Achiote* / Annato Oil
- 6 *Adobo*
- 7 *Ajili mójili*
- 8 *Escabeche*
- 9 *Mayoketchup*
- 10 *Mojito*
- 11 *Pique* / Hot Sauce
- 12 Salsa Criolla / Mojo Isleño / Creole Sauce
- 13 *Sofrito*

Section II. Fritters
- 15 Introduction
- 19 *Queso Frito* / Fried Cheese
- 21 *Pastelillos de Queso* / Cheese Turnovers
- 23 *Pastelillos de Guayaba* / Guava and Cheese Turnovers
- 24 *Pastelillos de Carne* / Meat Turnovers
- 25 *Frituras de Calabaza (Barrigas de Vieja)* / Pumpkin Fritters
- 27 *Chicharrones de Pollo* / Chicken Cracklings
- 29 *Sorullos (Saladitos)* / Salty Corn Stick Fritters
- 31 *Sorullos Dulces* / Sweet Corn Stick Fritters
- 33 *Bolitas de Queso* / Fried Cheese Balls
- 35 *Bacalaítos* / Salt Cod Fritters
- 37 *Buñuelos de Bacalao* / Salt Cod Cakes
- 39 *Almojábanas* / Rice Flour and Cheese Fritters
- 40 *Rellenos de Papa* / Stuffed Potato Fritters
- 41 *Alcapurrias* / Stuffed Yautía Fritters

Section III. Plantains and Roots
- 43 Introduction
- 45 *Platanutres* / Plantain Chips
- 47 *Tostones de Plátano* / Plantain "Tostones"
- 49 *Tostones de Pana* / Breadfruit "Tostones"
- 51 *Arañitas* / Plantain "Spiders"
- 53 *Amarillos en Almíbar* / Sweet Plantains in Syrup
- 55 *Mofongo de Amarillo* / Ripe Plantain Mofongo
- 57 *Mofongo de Plátano* / Green Plantain Mofongo
- 59 *Mofongo de Yuca* / Cassava Mofongo
- 61 *Viandas Majadas* / Mashed Root Vegetables
- 63 *Ensalada de Papa* / Potato Salad
- 65 *Piñón* / Ripe Plantain and Beef Lasagna
- 67 *Piononos* / Ripe Plantain and Beef Mold
- 68 *Pasteles* / Yautía and Pork Dumplings

Section IV. Soups and Stews

- 71 Introduction
- 72 *Caldo de Pollo Criollo* / Chicken Stock
- 73 *Caldo de Res* / Beef Stock
- 75 *Caldo de Pescado* / Fish Stock
- 77 *Sopa de Pollo y Fideos* / Chicken Noodle Soup
- 79 *Asopao de Pollo* / Chicken and Rice Soup
- 81 *Sopa de Viandas* / Root Vegetable Soup
- 83 *Sopa de Plátano* / Plantain Soup
- 85 *Sopa de Calabaza* / Caribbean Pumpkin Soup
- 87 *Berenjena Guisada* / Stewed Eggplant
- 89 *Guingambó Guisado* / Stewed Okra
- 91 Corned Beef
- 93 *Jamonilla Guisada* / Stewed Luncheon Meat
- 95 *Sancocho* / Root Vegetable and Beef Stew
- 97 *Fricasé de Pollo* / Chicken Stew
- 98 *Friscasé de Ternera* / Veal Stew
- 99 *Fricasé de Cabrito* / Stewed Goat
- 101 *Carne Guisada* / Beef Stew
- 103 *Patitas de Cerdo con Garbanzos* / Chickpea and Pig's Feet Stew
- 105 *Tasajo* / Salt Beef Stew

Section V. Rice, Grains, and Pasta

- 107 Introduction
- 111 *Arroz Blanco* / White Rice
- 113 *Arroz con Gandules* / Rice with Pigeon Peas
- 114 *Arroz con Garbanzos y Chorizo* / Rice with Chickpeas and Chorizo
- 115 *Arroz con Jamonilla* / Rice and Luncheon Meat
- 116 *Arroz con Maíz* / Rice with Corn
- 117 *Arroz con Jueyes* / Rice with Crabmeat
- 119 *Arroz con Longaniza* / Rice with Longaniza Sausage
- 121 *Arroz con Pollo* / Rice with Chicken
- 123 *Arroz con Salchichas* / Rice with Vienna Sausages
- 125 *Arroz Relleno* / Stuffed Rice
- 127 *Gandules con Bolitas de Plátano* / Pigeon Peas with Plantain Dumplings
- 129 *Garbanzos Guisados con Chorizo* / Strewed Chickpeas with Chorizo
- 131 *Habichuelas Blancas Guisadas* / Stewed White Beans
- 133 *Habichuelas Rojas Guisadas* / Stewed Red Kidney Beans
- 135 *Espagueti con Carne Criolla* / *Criollo* Style Spaghetti with Meat Sauce
- 137 *Espagueti con Pollo Criollo* / *Criollo* Style Spaghetti with Chicken
- 139 *Lasaña Criolla* / Puerto Rican Style Lasagna

Section VI. Meats

- 141 Introduction
- 143 *Sándwiches de Mezcla* / Luncheon Meat-mix
- 145 *Longaniza* / Criollo Pork Sausage
- 147 *Pollo al Horno* / Roast Chicken
- 149 *Pollo Frito* / Fried Chicken
- 151 *Pavo Criollo al Horno* / Puerto Rican-style Roast Turkey
- 153 *Chuletas Fritas* / Fried Pork Chops
- 155 *Pernil* / Roast Pork Butt
- 157 *Bistec Empanado* / Breaded Beef Cutlets

159 *Empanada Parmesana* / Breaded Beef Cutlets Parmesan
161 *Churrasco* / Skirt Steak
162 *Bistec Encebollado* / Beef Steaks with Onions
165 *Carne Frita* / Fried Pork
167 *Picadillo* / Spiced Ground Beef
169 *Chayotes Rellenos* / Stuffed Chayotes
171 *Queso Relleno* / Stuffed Cheese
172 *Jamón con Piña* / Ham with Pineapple Sauce
175 *Carne Mechada* / Stuffed Pot Roast

Section VII. Fish and Seafood
177 Introduction
180 *Ensalada de Carrucho* / Conch Salad
182 *Ensalada de Pulpo* / Octopus Salad
185 *Camarones al Ajillo* / Shrimp in Garlic Sauce
187 *Langosta al Ajillo* / Lobster with Garlic Sauce
189 *Salmorejo de Jueyes* / Crabmeat "Salmorejo"
190 *Serenata de Bacalao* / Salt Cod Salad with Root Vegetables
193 *Bacalao a la Vizcaína* / Baked Salt Cod Stew with Potatoes
195 *Funche con Bacalao* / Salt Cod Polenta
197 *Revoltillo con Bacalao* / Scrambled Eggs with Salt Cod
199 *Sierra en Escabeche* / Pickled Kingfish
201 *Chillo Frito* / Fried Red Snapper

Section VIII. Desserts
203 Introduction
205 *Dulce de Lechosa* / Candied Papaya
207 *Flan de Coco* / Coconut Custard
208 *Flan de Queso* / Cheese Custard
209 *Flan de Vainilla* / Vanilla Custard
211 *Budín de Pan* / Bread Pudding
213 *Arroz con Dulce* / Rice Pudding
215 *Tembleque* / Coconut Pudding
217 *Pastelillos de Guayaba* / Guava Pastries

Section IX. Step by Step
219 Introduction
220 *Pastelillos* / Turnovers
222 *Alcapurrias* / Stuffed *Yautía* Fritters
224 *Piononos* / *Yautía* and Pork Dumplings
226 *Pasteles* / *Yautía* and Pork Dumplings
228 *Arañitas* / Plantain "Spiders"
230 *Tostones* / Plantain "Tostones"
232 *Tostones con Tostonera* / Plantain "*Tostones*" with "*Tostonera*"
234 *Tostones Rellenos* / Plantain Stuffed "*Tostones*" with "*Tostonera*"
236 *Chillo Frito* / Fried Red Snapper
238 *Rellenos de Papa* / Stuffed Potato Fritters

240 ## Section X. Glossary

244 ## Section XI. Pictured Basics

246 ## Section XII. Index

About Myself

My story with food started when I was washing dishes for a living and recognized I had a calling for cooking. That's when I decided to do my first apprenticeship-on a non-paid basis, for an entire year-under Austrian, Swiss, Indian, Philippine, and local chefs at the Caribe Hilton Hotel in San Juan, in 1982.

From there, I attended the Culinary Institute of America in New York, graduating in the summer of 1985. I remained in New York for some years, working at Le Bernardin, The Maurice and The Water Club. My first job upon my return to Puerto Rico was as Chef de Cuisine for the Governor's Mansion, where my stint lasted for a couple of years... but my entrepreneurial thirst drove me, faster than I had planned, to start our own restaurant with my beloved wife, Lorraine.

Those were days of extreme hours of work, since we did everything ourselves with the help of a small staff and my parents-in-law, who took care of our oldest son, Gonzalo, while my parents placed their home on the line as collateral for our first loan. Other relatives and dear friends helped financially along the way, allowing us to achieve what is Pikayo Restaurant today, celebrating its 17th birthday.

It's not easy running a restaurant, which caused me to develop one of my most common daily phrases, "If it was just cooking, it would be a piece of cake."

Later, Lorraine would concentrate on our home and raising Gonzalo and Lucas, our youngest son, while I continued running the business, now with the help of a far greater staff of almost 100, spread between Pikayo; our latest restaurant, Payá; Museum Catering Services; and Museum Restaurant Group.

Many things happened along the way and through the years, in the form of consulting, special projects, running a cooking school, competitions, awards, and recognitions local and abroad, all contributing to enrich me and make me who I am today.

I feel I have been blessed in so many ways, for which I live eternally indebted and grateful to God.

Wilo Benet
San Juan, Puerto Rico
2007

Introduction

<u>Puerto Rico True Flavors</u> is a book intended to portray and facilitate the everyday culinary customs of Puerto Ricans in their homes and in local-fare restaurants, called *fondas*.

You will find, as you read, that this book contains a certain amount of recipes that I have developed which differ slightly from the originals. This is only to facilitate their preparation: I have been careful to guard and preserve their authenticity, integrity and flavors.

It is my strong suggestion that before you start any of the recipes in this book, you thoroughly read each from top to bottom: there will be crucial elements to their success that will require the use of tools, ingredients, or preparations that need to be arranged in advance. The recipes provided here have been triple-tested, to insure a high level of performance. However, as in any other area of life, "practice makes perfect," so some recipes may require practice in order to achieve their truest outcome.

As you collect information about food from any culture, you start to realize that different areas or regions may call equally-prepared recipes by totally different names, each unhesitating to stand by its choice rather than another region's version. Those names are embedded in us since childhood. Trying to influence anyone into accepting another name could end up in heated arguments, just like when talking about politics. In the majority of cases, I have chosen to use the recipe names from the northern coastline of Puerto Rico, which is where I was raised and lived most of my life.

Speaking of those years, I lived a very happy childhood in a home where my mother cooked from scratch for the family's breakfast, lunch and dinner, and my father barbecued often. This was complimented by both of my grandmothers, each of whom had specialties in their repertoires that to this day I still can't get over, remembering how great they were and which, along with my parent's cooking, were the first foundations of my love of food.

Another weighty element and one which is clearly depicted in this book, is the food served by the public school system, which also had a strong impact on what a lot of us feel is the true authentic everyday Puerto Rico fare.

Yet another influence is the culture of street food vendors, from fritter kiosks in the coastal areas to more modern stainless steel cart concoctions, with concepts spanning from *Bistec* Sandwiches to *Tripletas*; to rusty old wagons serving full-plate *Mixtas*; or roadside charcoal spit-roasted chickens, all of which are still ever-present and an integral part of everyday gastronomy here in Puerto Rico.

The photographic style I chose for this book is honest and unadorned. It does not contain any kind of decoration or propping for the shots, since my principal goal with the pictures is to provide the readers with a visual, up-close perspective, to better achieve the recipes here presented. Details and close-ups together propose that those dishes we have so much love for can also be represented in a more uniform way without ever compromising the authenticity of the recipes and the cultural heritage they represent.

I love and live proud to be Puerto Rican and feel that part of my mission in life is to do everything that is within my abilities and God-given talents to represent Puerto Rico and its gastronomy. My emotions are so strong and rooted on this subject that my keyboard is filled with tears of excitement, pride, joy and gratefulness for the opportunities that life has give me, as I write these lines.

Wilo Benet
San Juan, Puerto Rico
Spring 2007

pique sofrito mojito achiote
mayoketchup pique sofrito
mójili adobo escabeche ma
achiote ajili mójili adobo
pique sofrito mojito achiote
beche mayoketchup pique sof
mójili adobo escabeche may
mojito achiote ajili mójili
ayoketchup pique sofrito mojit
escabeche mayoketchup pique
hiote ajili mójili adobo esca
pique sofrito mojito achiote

Chapter I

Basics

Basics

This chapter's intentions are to take you through the very basic components in most of our recipes, which will include dry rubs, marinades and simple sauces that compliment many of the recipes.

Like any other culture there are some elements that define a culture's gastronomy and, in the case of Puerto Rico, *Sofrito* has got to be the single most widely used element.

Escabeche, which has evolved to be a sauce/vinaigrette from its original intention as a preserving method is a great example of a basic preparation's versatility, since it is used for a variety of recipes you will find throughout the book.

Another very common element is *Adobo* or dry rub which, to us, is as common as salt. In Puerto Rico, applying *adobo* is referred to as "*adobar*" and is considered a talent or gift when you can properly achieve intensity and flavor with it.

Our most basic flavor elements in general are *cilantro*, *culantro*, Spanish tomato sauce, olives, capers, onions, garlic, cubanelle peppers, sweet *ají* peppers, white vinegar, olive oil and sugar.

Many more elements are required to achieve True Puerto Rican cuisine but all of these basics are fundamental to the end result.

Aceite de Achiote

Annato Oil

Makes 6 cups

Ingredients:

- 1 gallon vegetable oil
- 1 pound *achiote* seeds

Procedure:

In a saucepan over medium-high heat, combine the vegetable oil with the *achiote* seeds. Cook for about 10 minutes without boiling, until the oil has been colored by the *achiote*. Remove from the heat, and steep for another 10 to 15 minutes. Drain, discard the remaining *achiote* seeds, and set the drained oil aside to cool. Pour into a container, and cover with a tight fitting lid. (No refrigeration is necessary).

Adobo

Dry Rub

Makes ½ cup

There are commercial brands of *adobo* seasoning available in the market, many with the addition of MSGs, from which I choose to refrain. Luckily, the ingredients in the mixture are available, so you can make your own *adobo* at home.

Ingredients:

- 3 tablespoons kosher salt
- 2 tablespoons Goya garlic powder
- 1 tablespoon Goya ground cumin
- ½ teaspoon freshly ground white pepper
- 1 teaspoon ground coriander or Goya oregano (optional)
- 2 tablespoons Goya onion powder

Procedure:

In a bowl, combine all the ingredients and mix. Store the *adobo* in a tightly sealed jar or bag, and keep in your cupboard.

Chapter I

Basics

Ajili mójili

Makes 2 cups

Ajili mójili is usually served as a dipping sauce for fritters, particularly *tostones* and *arañitas*. There are different versions throughout the island; I chose to make one that serves both as a dipping sauce or a spicy red *sofrito* to be added as a base for stewed beans and other typical dishes.

Ingredients:

- 1 cup Goya olive oil (not extra virgin), divided in half
- 7 *ajíes dulces*, seeds removed and roughly chopped
- 1 small onion, chopped
- 2 garlic cloves, peeled
- 3 *ajíes caballeros*, seeds removed
- 20 leaves *culantro*
- ½ cup fresh lime juice
- 2 tomatoes, peeled and seeds removed
- 2 teaspoons kosher salt
- ½ cup Goya Spanish tomato sauce
- ¼ teaspoon freshly ground black pepper
- 2 teaspoons sugar

Procedure:

1 In a high-sided skillet over medium-low heat, warm ½-cup of the olive oil. Add the *ajíes dulces* and the onion, and cook for about 2 minutes, or until the vegetables are soft and have lost their raw taste. Remove from the heat, and set aside to cool.

2 In a blender, combine the *ají*-onion mixture with the remaining ½-cup of olive oil, the garlic, *ajíes caballeros* and *culantro*. Process the mixture to obtain a coarse puree. Scrape the sides of the blender with a rubber spatula, add the lime juice, and process for another 30 seconds. Scrape the sides of the blender again, and process for another 30 seconds.

3 Add the tomatoes, season with the salt, and process for another 30 seconds. Add the tomato sauce, season with the black pepper and sugar, and process until a coarse-smooth, off-red puree with green speckles forms.

Escabeche, more than a recipe, is a pickling technique inherited from the Spaniards, and widely used throughout the Caribbean. Aside from the flavors this technique furnishes, it is also used as a preserving tool. This version of *escabeche*, which is widely served in Puerto Rico, is a simplified version of its original from Spain.

Cooked root vegetables, such as *yuca* or cooked green bananas, are traditionally steeped overnight in the *escabeche* in order to absorb the flavors from the vinegar, onion, peppercorns and bay leaves.

Escabeche

Pickling

Makes approximately 3 cups

Ingredients:

- 1½ cups Goya olive oil (not extra virgin)
- 1 large onion, julienne
- 3 garlic cloves, sliced into thin slivers
- 6 dried Goya bay leaves
- ½ teaspoon black peppercorns
- ½ cup white vinegar
- 1¼ tablespoons kosher salt

Procedure:

1 In a high-sided skillet over low heat, warm the olive oil. Add the onion, garlic slivers, bay leaves and peppercorns, and stir. Pour in the vinegar, season with the salt, and cook over low heat for about 12 minutes, stirring every 2 minutes.

2 Remove the *escabeche* from the heat and bring to room temperature.

3 At this point, cooked *yuca* or green bananas can be added, and set aside to steep in the *escabeche*, covered, for 8 to 24 hours.

The steeping time will determine the intensity of the flavors. If you can't count on 8 hours of steeping time, it is ok, just don't expect the flavor spectrum to be as evident.

Chapter I

Basics

Mayoketchup

Makes 1½ cups

This simple preparation is served as a dipping sauce for fried goodies such as *tostones* and *sorullitos*.

Ingredients:
- 1 cup mayonnaise
- ½ cup ketchup

Procedure:
In a bowl, combine the mayonnaise and the ketchup, and stir until a lump-free, pink mixture forms.

Variations:

1 For a tangier version of the sauce, stir in 2 tablespoons of finely chopped capers.

2 For a more pungent version, sauté one teaspoon of minced garlic in 1 tablespoon of olive oil over low heat. Set aside to cool, and stir into the *mayoketchup*.

3 For a saltier, more complex flavor, sprinkle the *mayoketchup* with ½ teaspoon (or 1 teaspoon if you have a high tolerance to salty things) of powdered *adobo* (see recipe on page 6).

4 A dash of Puerto Rican-style *pique* or any other hot sauce add piquancy to the traditional dipping sauce.

Garlic Mojito

Makes 2 cups

Garlic Mojito is traditionally served as a dressing for large pieces of cooked root vegetables. *Yuca* is the most common one used in this preparation. The dressing lends flavor and moisture to the root, whose fibrous texture perfectly absorbs the flavored oil.

This recipe makes enough *mojito* to dress two large *yucas*, which provide for six generous portions.

Ingredients:

- 1½ cups Goya olive oil (not extra virgin)
- 1 large onion, julienne
- 3 cloves garlic, sliced into thin slivers
- 1 tablespoon kosher salt
- ¼ cup vinegar

Procedure:

In a sauté pan over medium-low heat, warm the olive oil. Add the onion and garlic slivers, season with the salt, and cook for about 12 minutes, stirring occasionally. Add the vinegar. It is important to cook the onions slowly, so that no browning occurs. The ultimate goal is to cook the onion evenly until it becomes soft and translucent and it has released all its sweetness into the oil.

Garlic Mojito can also be served as a dipping sauce for *tostones*. In this case, finely dice the onion, and cook according to the standard recipe. This could be a good exercise for those who want to practice their dexterity in the brunoise cut.

Chapter I

Basics

Pique

Hot Sauce

Makes about 2 ½ cups

Traditionally, *pique* is a vinegar-based homemade hot sauce commonly stored in a small rum bottle or *caneca*. I added oil because it helps carry the flavors from all the ingredients and it coats the mouth when flavoring the hot sauce, soothing the palate to provide a more mellow experience.

Ingredients:

- 20 ajíes *caballeros*
- 10 leaves *culantro*
- 10 cloves garlic
- 3 ounces ripe pineapple rind
- 2 tablespoons salt
- 1 tablespoon sugar
- 2 cups white vinegar
- ¼ cup vegetable oil
- ¼ cup Goya olive oil (not extra virgin)

Procedure:

1. Split the *ajíes caballeros* in half lengthwise so that the seeds are exposed during the fermentation process. Drop the *ajíes* into a 16-ounce glass jar or bottle (with a tight fitting lid or cork), and add the *culantro*, garlic and pineapple rind.

2. Using a funnel, pour the salt, sugar, vinegar and vegetable and olive oils into the jar and seal tightly. Shake well and set aside to ferment in a cool place for at least one week. (*Pique* does not need to be refrigerated).

Be aware of the possibility of having the garlic turn color. The contact with vinegar, or any other acidic ingredient, creates a chemical reaction that makes garlic cloves turn blue. This does not affect its taste or edibility.

Salsa Criolla

Mojo Isleño / Creole Sauce
Makes 4 cups

Ingredients:

- ⅓ cup Goya olive oil (not extra virgin)
- 1 medium onion, diced
- 1 cubanelle pepper, seeds and inner white ribbings removed, diced
- 3 garlic cloves, sliced into thin slivers
- ½ teaspoon kosher salt
- ½ cup *sofrito* (see recipe on page 13)
- ⅓ cup tomato paste
- 2½ cups Goya Spanish tomato sauce
- ¼ cup sugar
- ⅓ cup Goya capers, drained
- ⅓ cup chopped *cilantro*
- ¾ cup white vinegar
- 6 Goya bay leaves
- ⅓ cup chopped *culantro*

Procedure:

1. In a large sauté pan over medium-high heat, warm the olive oil. Add the onion, cubanelle pepper and garlic slivers, season with the salt and cook, stirring, for about 2 minutes until the vegetables begin to soften.

2. Stir in the *sofrito* and cook, stirring, for another 2 minutes, at which time the aroma in your kitchen should have you buying plane tickets to Puerto Rico, if you're not already here!

3. Stir in the tomato paste, tomato sauce and sugar. Add the capers and *cilantro* and stir in the vinegar. Add the bay leaves and stir, being careful not to break the leaves. Lower the heat and cook, stirring every 2 minutes until the sauce has reduced, the red color has intensified, and the flavors have concentrated, about 15 minutes. The sauce should cook over low heat so that a scattered occasional bubbling occurs. Slow cooking and occasionally stirring the *mojo* will prevent the tomato sauce and the sugar to over-caramelize, inadvertently scorching the bottom of the pan. Remove from the heat, and stir in the *culantro*.

Chapter I

Basics

Sofrito

Makes 3 cups

Ingredients:

- ¼ cup Goya olive oil (not extra virgin)
- ½ cup vegetable oil
- 1 medium onion, roughly chopped
- 12 garlic cloves, peeled
- ~~3 cubanelle peppers~~ *Green bell peppers*, seeds and inner white ribbings removed, roughly chopped
- ~~10 ajíes dulces~~ seeds removed and roughly chopped
- 1 bunch *cilantro* (leaves and tender stems only)
- 30 leaves ~~culantro~~ *cilantro / parsley*
- ½ cup fresh oregano (leaves only), loosely packed

Procedure:

1 In a blender, combine the olive oil with the vegetable oil. Add the onion and garlic and process for about 30 seconds to obtain a pungent white purée.

2 Add the cubanelle peppers and the *ajíes dulces*, and blend for another 30 seconds to obtain a light-green purée. Add the *cilantro*, *culantro* and oregano. Pulse, and once finished, scrape the sides of the blender with a rubber spatula. Process for another 30 seconds to obtain an herbed-speckled light-green purée with a piquant taste and a pungent aroma.

At this point, the *sofrito* can be used as a condiment base for numerous recipes, from soups to stews, or it can be sealed in a jar and kept in the freezer for up to one month.

Dividing the *sofrito* into smaller portions or pouring the mixture into ice trays and tightly sealing them with plastic wrap are great ways to have portion-size access to the sofrito.

(Because *sofrito* serves as a base for numerous recipes, no salt should be added to the mixture.)

frituras chicharrones **sorullos** b
calaítos buñuelos **almojába**
s rellenos de papa **pastelillos** f
es sorullos **bolitas de queso** bac
mojábanas alcapurrias **rellenos**
frituras chicharrones **sorullos** b
calaítos buñuelos **almojába**
s rellenos de papa **pastelillos** f
es sorullos **bolitas de queso** bac
mojábanas alcapurrias **rellenos**
frituras chicharrones **sorullos** b
calaítos buñuelos **almojába**

Chapter II

Fritters

Fritters

Culturally, most Puerto Ricans have a love affair with fritters. I don't know its exact roots, but one thing I'm certain of: we love everything that is fried. Even when dieting, the temptation to eat fried food is often stronger than our will.

In my opinion fritters are an art form; one that takes as long to master as any other. If you fry them too long, they can become bitter or too hard; if they are fried too little, they become oily and soggy. But there is nothing like a perfectly fried fritter, crispy and light at the same time, which we refer to as *volao*, for a fabulous, perfect texture.

Although there are fritters all over the island, the kiosks out in Luquillo and Loíza are the perfect setting for a fritter experience. For the visiting traveler, this may be a little more adventurous than originally bargained for, because the setting is rustic and down-right local. Visually it may make one hesitant, since the large steel *calderos* (with a wood-burning fire under them) contain oil or lard (and only God knows when it was last changed), but certainly for what we Puerto Ricans consider a classical fritter, that oil has to be making some flavor contributions.

When you go by these kiosks, or shacks, on the side of the road, the sights and smells are unique. For instance, the sights are those of bunches of cod fritters or *bacalaítos* all held together with a wire, laid right on top of the *calderos* and being cooked by the wood-burning fire. Local palates water in anticipation from the smells of burning wood and cooking *bacalaítos*, since it is present in the air for miles preceding the kiosks. Regardless of social status, people from very different walks of life make a stop at these kiosks to indulge in our love affair with fritters.

Just like any other culture, the inclusion of certain elements in any given day or occasion is part of the authenticity. Fritters are one of those. No party is a party without fritters, or *piscolabis*, which is our local word for hors d'oeuvres whether they are fried or not.

Take for instance, the *pastelillo*, or turnover as it is called in America. (And more recently, *empanada*, a word with Argentinean roots, which to us locally means a whole other thing: a breaded cutlet.) *Pastelillos* are yellow or white dough pockets filled with everything under the sky, but the absolute classics are beef and cheese.

Another of these inherited ingredients that has now become a cultural staple is the mixture of equal parts of mayonnaise and ketchup - Yes, ketchup! - for dipping the fritters, which is referred to as *mayoketchup*. Some places add garlic, others add herbs, and so on, to personalize the sauce, but in the end it is what it is. It baffles me why we do not make more frequent use of sauces which are truly ours, and perfect mates for those fritters, like *ajili mójili*, which is a much more flavorful and authentic choice.

When any of these fritters are made in miniature size, we say they are *para picar* or *picadera* which literally translates as "to chop" but for us it means they are "to nibble on".

15

(continued)

Most classical fritters of our culture, such as *alcapurrias*, *pastelillos*, *bacalaítos* and many others comprise full-fledged industries since the work involved in making them is tedious and artisan-like. These versions will hardly represent the true efforts of our culture's best cooks, who will spend a sensational amount of time and work with very little remuneration to produce the real thing, but I suspect the appreciation for the product, in the form of praise, may entirely displace the need for just economic exchange.

There are other fritters, such as *tostones*, which have evolved over time to become hors d'oeuvres, but in their true traditional use were always sought after as side dishes to main courses. You will discover throughout this book that our culture is more about double starch and protein rather than including a greater amount of vegetables.

In my opinion, there is only one perfect time to pick green plantains for making *tostones* and that is when they are unquestionably green. They must be flattened very thin and fried until crispy, as opposed to other popular versions where the preference is that of a plantain that is not entirely green and thus does not allow the fried plantains to become very crispy.

The evolution of this fritter from side dish to *piscolabis* happened in my generation, when there was a proliferation of molds and pressing devices to form the *tostones* in ways that allow them to be stuffed with everything imaginable. Then came other classics, such as *tostones* with caviar which, when properly prepared, can be fabulous substitutions for toast points or even *blinis*, if you should want to consume caviar Caribbean-style. This perfect marriage is all due to the salt content of caviar, since *tostones* need to be salted generously.

There are other fritters that, despite any efforts, cannot be commercialized. My favorite ones are *almojábanas*, made with rice flour and Farmers cheese. With the right recipe, the perfect oil temperature, and applied frying skills these fritters can be downright addictive.

Considering new ideas is a wonderful human experience, and the process of their evolution even more enjoyable. I am referring to what I think is a local modern classic, at least in the mind of most of my customers at Pikayo (www.pikayo.com). This patron-proclaimed classic I call *Tostones de Arroz Pegao*. Let me start by explaining *pegao*, which is what settles at the bottom of a pot of rice and becomes very crispy. In our culture, this is scraped from the pot and sprinkled over the moist rice to create a texture contrast with its crunch. From that point, what I did was expand the concept and, with a totally different process further than just scraping pots of rice for their crispy bottoms, I created *Tostones de Arroz Pegao*, which is the signature *piscolabis* at Pikayo (www.pikayo.com). Essentially, what it turns out to be is a small flattened bundle of very crispy rice, the size of a quarter but slightly thicker, which serves as the base for a bounty of local or international possibilities. The most popular topping is Tuna Tartar with Chipotle Chile Sauce, followed by Land Crab *Salmorejo;* Foie Gras Terrine and Black Truffle Honey; Octopus Salad; and Prosciutto and Parmesan, to name just a few.

In this chapter, you will experience a few of the recipes which I feel best represent the true flavors of our culture when the subject is fritters.

Chapter II

Fritters

Queso Frito

Fried Cheese

Makes 32 cheese cubes

Ingredients:

- 12 ounces *queso fresco del país**
- ¼ cup flour
- vegetable oil for frying

Procedure:

1. Cut the cheese in half crosswise to end up with two 1-inch-thick squares. Cut each square into quarters, and cube. Place the flour in a bowl, add the cheese cubes, and toss to dredge lightly.

2. In a frying pan or deep fryer, heat about 3 inches of vegetable oil to 350° F. Carefully drop the cheese into the hot oil, and fry for about 2 minutes, or until the edges of the cheese cubes are lightly browned. Remove from the oil, and drain on paper towels. Serve immediately.

*Queso Frito, served as an appetizer with some sliced, sautéed *chorizo* makes a beautiful marriage. If you can't get Puerto Rico cheese, you may try this recipe with Mexican *queso fresco*.

Chapter II

Fritters

Pastelillos de Queso

Cheese Turnovers

Makes about 2 dozen

Ingredients:
- 1 package 6" *plantilla* rounds (turnover dough)
- 24 slices standard American cheese
- vegetable oil for frying

See step-by-step procedure on page 220

Procedure:

Before starting, set up a comfortable workspace to prepare the *pastelillos*. While you work, keep the *plantillas* covered with a damp kitchen towel to keep them from drying out. A moist *plantilla* facilitates the sealing of the *pastelillo*. If necessary, keep a small bowl of water handy to moisten the edges of the *pastelillo* when sealing

1 Place a *plantilla* on a clean flat surface. Cut a slice of cheese into strips, and arrange over half of the *plantilla*. Using the tip of your finger lightly paint the edges of the *plantilla* with water. Fold the *plantilla* over the cheese to form a half-moon-shaped *pastelillo*, and press the edges firmly together to seal. With the back of a fork, lightly crimp the edges of the *pastelillo* on both sides. With the tips of your fingers, press gently on the crimped edges of the *pastelillos*, to secure the sealing. (If the dough breaks, pinch and seal it with your fingers, otherwise start over with a new *plantilla*; holes in the dough will cause the *pastelillo* to absorb excess oil and the filling to come out during frying). Repeat with the remaining *plantillas* and cheese, and set the *pastelillos* aside.

2 In a frying pan, heat about 2 inches of vegetable oil to 350°F. Add the *pastelillos*, in batches, to the hot oil, and fry for 1 to 2 minutes on each side, or until golden. Remove from the oil, set aside to drain on paper towels, and serve immediately.

Aside from being a great snack, *pastelillos* make for great appetizers or finger food. It's all a matter of getting creative with the dough. For a family style appetizer platter, make triangle-shaped *pastelillos*. Simply cut the *plantillas* in half, add 1 tablespoon of filling, and fold each half into triangles. Seal and fry as specified. For a smaller treat, use a 2-inch cookie cutter to divide the *plantillas* into 3 smaller rounds. Arrange ¼ slice of cheese on one side of each round, and fold into little half-moons. Seal the edges, crimp with a fork, and fry. The authentic look of the dough, once fried, will be blistered.

Served in many *merenderos* (lunch stands) throughout the island, these *pastelillos* are a kid's beloved lunch item.

PUERTO RICO TRUE FLAVORS BY WILO BENET

Pastelillos de Guayaba

Guava and Cheese Turnovers
Makes about 2 dozen

Chapter II

Fritters

Ingredients:
- 1 package 6" *plantilla* rounds (turnover dough)
- 8 ounces cream cheese
- 8 ounces guava paste
- vegetable oil for frying

See step-by-step procedure on page 220

Procedure:

Before starting, set up a comfortable workspace to prepare the *pastelillos*. While you work, keep the *plantillas* covered with a damp kitchen towel to keep them from drying out. A moist *plantilla* facilitates the sealing of the *pastelillo*. If necessary, keep a small bowl of water handy to moisten the edges of the *pastelillo* when sealing.

1 Place a *plantilla* on a clean flat surface, and drop 1 tablespoon each of cream cheese and guava paste onto half of the *plantilla*. Using the tip of your finger lightly paint the edges of the *plantilla* with water. Fold the *plantilla* over the filling to form a half-moon-shaped *pastelillo*, and press the edges firmly together to seal. With the back of a fork, lightly crimp the edges of the *pastelillo* on both sides. With the tips of your fingers, press gently on the crimped edges of the *pastelillos*, to secure the sealing. (If the dough breaks, pinch and seal it with your fingers, otherwise start over with a new *plantilla*; holes in the dough will cause the *pastelillo* to absorb excess oil and the filling to come out during frying). Repeat with the remaining *plantillas*, cream cheese and guava paste, and set the *pastelillos* aside.

2 In a frying pan, heat about 2 inches of vegetable oil to 350° F. Add the *pastelillos*, in batches, to the hot oil, and fry for 1 to 2 minutes on each side, or until golden. Remove from the oil, set aside to drain on paper towels. Allow these *pastelillos* to cool slightly before biting into them. The steam from the melted guava can be lethal to impatient lips.

Aside from being a great snack, *pastelillos* make for great appetizers or finger food. It's all a matter of getting creative with the dough. For a family style appetizer platter, make triangle-shaped *pastelillos*. Simply cut the *plantillas* in half, add 1 tablespoon of filling, and fold each half into triangles. Seal and fry as specified. For a smaller treat, use a 2-inch cookie cutter to divide the *plantillas* into 3 smaller rounds. Add ½ teaspoon each of cream cheese and guava paste, and fold into little half-moons. Seal the edges, crimp with a fork, and fry. The authentic look of the dough, once fried, will be blistered.

Pastelillos de Carne

Meat Turnovers
Makes about 2 dozen

Ingredients:
- 1 package 6" *plantilla* rounds (*pastelillo* dough/turnover dough)
- 1 ½ cups *picadillo* (see recipe on page 167)
- vegetable oil for frying

See step-by-step procedure on page 220

Procedure:

Before starting, set up a comfortable workspace to prepare the *pastelillos*. While you work, keep the *plantillas* covered with a damp kitchen towel to keep them from drying out. A moist *plantilla* facilitates the sealing of the *pastelillo*. If necessary, keep a small bowl of water handy to moisten the edges of the pastelillo when sealing.

1 Place a *plantilla* on a clean flat surface, and drop 2 tablespoons of *picadillo* onto half of the *plantilla*. Using the tip of your finger lightly paint the edges of the *plantilla* with water. Fold the *plantilla* over the filling to form a half-moon-shaped *pastelillo*, and press the edges firmly together to seal. With the back of a fork, lightly crimp the edges of the *pastelillo* on both sides. With the tips of your fingers, press gently on the crimped edges of the *pastelillos*, to secure the sealing. (If the dough breaks, pinch and seal it with your fingers, otherwise start over with a new *plantilla*; holes in the dough will cause the *pastelillo* to absorb excess oil and the filling to come out during frying). Repeat with the remaining *plantillas* and *picadillo*.

2 In a frying pan, heat about 2 inches of vegetable oil to 350° F. Add the *pastelillos*, in batches, to the hot oil, and fry for 1 to 2 minutes on each side, or until golden. Remove from the oil, set aside to drain on paper towels, and serve immediately.

Aside from being a great snack, *pastelillos* make great appetizers or finger food. It's all a matter of getting creative with the dough. For a family style appetizer platter, make triangle-shaped *pastelillos*. Simply cut the *plantillas* in half, add 1 tablespoon of filling, and fold each half into triangles. Seal and fry as specified. For a smaller treat, use a 2-inch cookie cutter to divide the *plantillas* into 3 smaller rounds. Add 1 teaspoon of *picadillo*, and fold into little half-moons. Seal the edges, crimp with a fork, and fry. The authentic look of the dough, once fried, will be blistered.

Chapter II

Fritters

Frituras de Calabaza
(Barrigas de Vieja)

Pumpkin Fritters
Makes 2 dozen

Ingredients:

- 1 pound mashed *calabaza* (Caribbean Pumpkin) (or substitute 2 cups pumpkin purée)
- 1 egg, beaten
- 1 teaspoon Goya ground cinnamon
- ½ teaspoon Goya ground cloves
- 6 tablespoons sugar
- ½ teaspoon kosher salt
- 1 cup all-purpose flour
- vegetable oil for frying

Procedure:

1. In a bowl, combine the mashed *calabaza* with the egg, cinnamon, cloves, sugar and salt, and mix well. Fold in the flour to obtain a thick smooth batter.

2. In a frying pan, heat about 1 inch of vegetable oil to 350°F. Carefully drop tablespoonfuls of the *calabaza* batter, in batches, into the hot oil, and fry for about 5 minutes. Remove from the oil, drain on paper towels, and serve.

Despite the fact that these are fritters, they are not intended to have a crisp texture. Nonetheless, you shouldn't discard them from the hors d'oeuvres selection at your next Caribbean-themed cocktail party. The evident spice element makes them a delicious, down-home snack.

These fritters are commonly known as *Barrigas de Vieja* or "old ladies' bellies". Like many things in our culture, the reason why they're called that remains somewhat of a mystery, although the concave shape the fritter acquires once it hits the hot oil might have something to do with it.

If I was my grandmother, I would hack away at the chicken, with no concern for equal-sized pieces that would cook more evenly and serve as more appealing eye candy. Nevertheless, one of my intentions for this cookbook is not only to present a current appreciation for the truest Puerto Rican home cooking, but to contribute in some way to standardizing it and actualizing it to the necessities of today's home cooks.

What sets Puerto Rican fried chicken apart from American recipes is the omission of flour products; we rely solely on the chicken's skin for crispness. Before there were chicken nuggets and to this day, *Chicharrones de Pollo* (chicken cracklings) remain our children's favored form of fried chicken.

Chapter II

Fritters

Chicharrones de Pollo

Chicken Cracklings
Serves 4 to 6

Ingredients:

- 1 whole chicken, about 4 pounds, innards removed
- 3 tablespoons *adobo* (see recipe on page 6)
- 2 tablespoons garlic that has been pounded to a paste
- 1 tablespoon *sofrito* (see recipe on page 13)
- 2 tablespoons Goya olive oil (not extra virgin)
- 3 tablespoons white vinegar
- vegetable oil for frying

Procedure:

1 Separate the chicken into parts: With a knife, remove the wings, thighs and drumsticks from the chicken, and set aside. Cut away the drummettes, cut and discard the joint bone, and set aside. Cut out the chicken's backbone entirely (discard or reserve for chicken stock if desired). Split the breast in two, and set aside.

2 With a cleaver, split each breast in half lengthwise, and cut each piece into 4 even-sized pieces, careful to keep the skin as intact as possible, and set aside. Cut and discard the joint bone from the drumsticks, cut the drumsticks in two, and set aside. Remove the central bone from the thighs, and cut each thigh into 6 parts, careful to keep the skin intact.

3 Place the chicken pieces in a bowl. Add the *adobo*, garlic paste, *sofrito*, olive oil and vinegar, and toss to completely coat the chicken pieces. Cover and set aside in the refrigerator to marinate overnight.

4 In a deep fryer, heat about 4 inches of vegetable oil to 350°F. Add the chicken pieces, initially stirring to prevent them from sticking to one another. Fry for 10 to 15 minutes until they achieve a deep golden brown color. Remove from the oil, and drain on paper towels. Serve warm.

Chapter II

Fritters

Sorullos (Saladitos)

Salty Corn Stick Fritters

Yields about 40

Ingredients:

- ½ teaspoon salt
- ½ teaspoon nutmeg
- 2 tablespoons melted butter
- 1½ cups grated Parmigiano-Reggiano (or substitute domestic Parmesan)
- 1½ cups fine cornmeal
- vegetable oil for frying

Procedure:

1 In a saucepan over medium-high heat, bring 2 cups of water to a boil with the salt, nutmeg and butter. Add the cheese and the cornmeal, and stir vigorously with a wooden spoon until the dough pulls away from the sides of the saucepan and forms a ball. Remove from the heat, and set aside to cool slightly.

2 Once the dough is cool enough to handle with your hands, transfer to a clean flat surface. Using your hands, roll the dough into 4-inch long by ½-inch-thick cylinders. I also suggest a nontraditional but reliable method to shape the *sorullos*: flatten the dough into a 12" x 8" rectangle. Dip a sharp knife in water, and run lengthwise through the middle of the rectangle (you should be left with 2 rectangles). Cut each rectangle into 4-inch-long by ½-inch-thick sticks.

3 In a frying pan or deep fryer, heat about 3 inches of vegetable oil to 350°F. Drop the *sorullos* into the hot oil, in batches, and fry until crisp and golden brown, about 8 minutes. Remove from the oil, and drain on paper towels. Serve immediately with *mayoketchup* (recipe on page 9) on the side for dipping.

As in many cultures, we have inherited a variety of products from others. Puerto Rican cuisine seems to be keen on Parmesan cheese which, in the case of *sorullos*, blends quite well with the cornmeal to provide the fritters with an incomparable crisp texture.

Chapter II

Fritters

Sorullos Dulces

Sweet Corn Stick Fritters
Makes 10

Ingredients:

- 2 teaspoons kosher salt
- ½ cup sugar
- 2 tablespoons melted butter
- 2 cups fine cornmeal
- vegetable oil for frying

Procedure:

1 In a saucepan over medium-high heat, bring 2 cups of water to a boil with the salt, sugar and butter. Add the cornmeal, and stir vigorously with a wooden spoon until the dough begins to pull away from the sides of the saucepan and forms a ball. Remove from the heat, and set aside to cool slightly.

2 Once the dough is cool enough to handle with your hands, but still warm and pliable, use your hands to roll the dough into 2" x ½" cylinders. Flatten the sides with your fingers.

3 In a frying pan or deep fryer, heat about 3 inches of vegetable oil to 350°F. Drop the *sorullos* into the hot oil, in batches, and fry until crisp and golden brown, about 12 minutes. Remove from the oil, and drain on paper towels. Serve immediately.

Play around with this recipe by stuffing the *sorullos* with some American or Velveeta cheese.

> Chapter II
>
> Fritters

Bolitas de Queso

Fried Cheese Balls

Makes 3 dozen

Ingredients:

For the cheese balls:
- 1 pound Edam cheese, shredded
- 2 egg whites
- 6 tablespoons all-purpose flour, plus extra for dredging
- vegetable oil for frying

For the guava sauce:
- 7 ounces guava paste
- ⅓ cup white vinegar
- 1 tablespoon chopped *cilantro*
- ¼ cup of water

Procedure:

1 Prepare the guava sauce: In a small saucepan over medium-high heat, combine the guava paste with the vinegar and a half-cup of water. Using a whisk, break down the guava paste, and cook until it dissolves into a smooth sauce, about 4 minutes. Remove the sauce from the heat, and stir in the *cilantro*. Set aside to cool to room temperature.

2 Prepare the dough: Place the shredded cheese in the bowl of a standing mixer, and with the paddle attachment, beat on medium speed until the cheese pulls away from the edges of the bowl and forms a ball. Add the egg whites, and mix until they incorporate into the cheese. Add 6 tablespoons of flour, and mix until a unified dough forms. Refrigerate the dough for about 30 minutes to facilitate the shaping of the balls.

3 Scoop out a tablespoon of the dough, and using the palms of your hands, roll it into a small ball. Repeat with the remaining dough, and set the cheese balls aside.

4 In a frying pan, or deep fryer, heat about 3 inches of vegetable oil to 350°F. Dredge the cheese balls in flour, patting off any excess, and carefully drop them, in batches, into the hot oil. Fry for 2 to 3 minutes until golden brown. Using a slotted spoon, remove the cheese balls from the oil, and set aside to drain on paper towels. Serve immediately with the guava sauce for dipping.

Chapter II

Fritters

Bacalaítos

Salt Cod Fritters
Makes 1 dozen

Ingredients:
- 12 ounces salt cod fillet, soaked overnight and drained
- 1¾ cups all-purpose flour
- 1 tablespoon baking powder
- 1 tablespoon *adobo* (see recipe on page 6)
- 2 tablespoons chopped *cilantro*

Procedure:

1. Clean the salt cod: Remove any small bones and any tough skin from the salt cod, and coarsely shred the fillet into a bowl.

2. Add the flour, baking powder, *adobo* and *cilantro* to the bowl, and pour in 3 cups of water. Mix well until a chunky, unified batter that resembles pancake batter forms.

3. In a large frying pan, heat about 1 inch of vegetable oil to 350°F. Using a 2-ounce ladle and with a forward motion, pour the batter, in batches, into the hot oil, to form an elongated, flat fritter. Fry for about 10 minutes, turning occasionally with tongs, until crisp and golden brown. If the fritters happen to stick to the bottom of the pan while frying, use a thin spatula to detach them. Oil bubbling through the fritter during frying is a good indication of a perfectly fried *bacalaíto*.

4. Remove the *bacalaítos* from the oil, and set aside to drain on paper towels.

Because these fritters are extremely oily, I recommend standing them in a colander or placing them over a cooling rack to drain before serving. Serve immediately.

Probably the epitome of Puerto Rico's fritter, *bacalaítos* are still cooked in their original rustic form along the island's coast.

Buñuelos de Bacalao

Salt Cod Cakes
Makes 3 dozen

Chapter II

Fritters

Ingredients:

- 14 ounces salt cod fillet*
- 2 cups milk
- 1 tablespoon Goya olive oil (not extra virgin)
- 2 tablespoons *sofrito* (see recipe on page 13)
- 1¼ cups Goya Spanish tomato sauce
- 3 *ajíes dulces*, seeds removed and minced
- ¼ cup finely chopped fresh oregano
- 1½ cups self-rising cake flour, sifted
- vegetable oil for frying

Procedure:

1 Reconstitute the salt cod: Place the salt cod in a deep dish, and cover with the milk and 2 cups of water. Cover, and set aside in the refrigerator to soak overnight. The milk acts as a tenderizer for a silkier texture and a more tender bite.

2 Drain the salt cod, and carefully remove any small bones or tough skin that remains. At this point you should be left with about 12 ounces of fillet.

3 Cut the fillet into chunks, and combine them in a saucepan with 2 cups of water and the olive oil. Bring to a slow simmer (do not boil or the fish will toughen), and cook for about 6 minutes.

4 Drain the water from the saucepan, and using a fork, flake the salt cod. Return the saucepan with the salt cod to medium-low heat, and add the *sofrito*, tomato sauce, *ajíes* and oregano. Cook, stirring to obtain a thick stew, about 4 minutes. Remove the stew from the heat, stir in 1 cup of water, and set aside to cool. (To speed the cooling process, spread the stew on a sheet pan and refrigerate for 15 to 20 minutes).

5 Prepare the batter: Transfer the stew to a bowl, and slowly fold in the flour, scraping the sides of the bowl with a rubber spatula to make sure all the flour is worked into the stew. The resulting batter should have a chunky consistency and should be thick enough that when a fork is run through its surface, a streak is left behind.

6 In a frying pan, or deep fryer, heat about 3 inches vegetable oil to 350°F. Carefully drop tablespoonsful or small (#70) ice cream scoopfuls of the batter, in batches, into the hot oil. Fry for 2 to 3 minutes until golden brown, turning occasionally to make sure the fritters brown evenly.

7 Using a slotted spoon, remove the *buñuelos* from the oil, and set aside to drain on paper towels. Serve immediately.

*A thicker salt cod fillet will be representative of a better quality and will provide for a silkier texture.

> **Chapter II**
>
> Fritters

Almojábanas

Rice Flour and Cheese Fritters

Makes 2 dozen

Ingredients:

- 2 cups milk
- 1 teaspoon kosher salt
- 2 cups enriched rice flour
- 5 eggs
- 12 ounces *queso fresco del país*, crumbled
- vegetable oil for frying

Procedure:

1 In a round-edged saucepan over medium heat, bring the milk to a boil, and stir in the salt. Add the rice flour, and stir vigorously with a wooden spoon, until the mixture pulls away from the sides of the pan and forms a ball. Transfer to a bowl, and set aside to cool slightly.

2 Once the dough has cooled to the point where you can handle it with your hands, incorporate the eggs (one by one) into the dough to form a thick smooth batter. At this point, incorporate the crumbled cheese.

3 In a frying pan, or a deep fryer, heat about 3 inches of vegetable oil to 350°F. Carefully drop tablespoonfuls of the *almojábana* batter, in batches, into the hot oil. Fry for 2 to 3 minutes until golden brown, turning occasionally to make sure the fritters brown evenly.

4 Using a slotted spoon, remove the *almojábanas* from the oil, and set aside to drain on paper towels. Serve immediately.

Almojábanas are a traditional family treat. Because their taste is a bit neutral, they are commonly served drizzled with honey or pancake syrup or served as a dipping treat for hot chocolate.

Rellenos de Papa

Stuffed Potato Fritters
Makes 2 dozen

Ingredients:

- 6 large Idaho potatoes, peeled
- ¼ kosher salt
- 2 tablespoons Goya olive oil (not extra virgin)
- ¾ cup *picadillo* (see recipe on page 167)
- 4 ounces cream cheese
- cornstarch for dredging
- vegetable oil for frying

See step-by-step procedure on page 238

To this day, I clearly remember when my height just barely allowed me to look over the countertop of our kitchen, and see the results of my mother's labors when she had prepared Rellenos de Papa for us. It was a procedure that took her all morning.

Had those prepared rellenos already been fried, I would have cheated on waiting for dinnertime, and eaten them right on the spot!

Procedure:

1. Boil the potatoes: Place the whole potatoes in a large pot, add enough cold water to cover, and bring to a boil. It is important to keep the potatoes whole while boiling so that they conserve the level of starchiness necessary for the shaping of the *rellenos*. Add ¼ cup of salt to the boiling water, and cook for about 45 minutes, until the potatoes are fork-tender.

2. Drain the potatoes. While still hot, break the potatoes down with a masher or a wire whisk until free of large lumps, but not completely smooth. Season the mashed potatoes with 1 teaspoon of salt, and set aside to cool until they are easier to handle with your hands.

3. Prepare the *rellenos*: Dip a #22 ice cream scoop in water, and tightly pack it with the mashed potatoes. Dip your forefinger in olive oil, and press into the center of the potatoes to make a cavity, without reaching all the way through. Rotate your finger inside to widen the cavity. Stuff the cavity with 1 teaspoon of *picadillo* and ½ teaspoon of cream cheese, and press down gently.

4. Release the stuffed dumpling into your hand, and carefully seal the cavity by folding the mashed potatoes over it. (Make sure that it is evenly sealed to ensure that no stuffing leaks out when frying the *rellenos*). Gently roll the dumpling into a smooth ball. Repeat with the remaining mashed potatoes, meat and cheese. (Remember to dip the ice cream scoop in water before packing it with the mashed potatoes, so that the dumplings release themselves easily).

5. In a frying pan, heat about 3 inches of vegetable oil to 350°F. Dredge the *rellenos de papa* in cornstarch, patting off any excess. Using a slotted spoon, carefully lower them into the hot oil. Fry for 3 to 4 minutes, turning occasionally if necessary, until golden.

6. Using a slotted spoon, remove the *rellenos* from the oil, and set aside to drain on paper towels. Serve immediately.

Chapter II

Fritters

Alcapurrias

Stuffed *Yautía* Fritters
Makes 2 dozen

Ingredients:

- 2 pounds *yautía*
- ¼ cup *achiote* oil
  (see recipe on page 6)
- 2 tablespoons *adobo*
  (see recipe on page 6)
- ¾ cup *picadillo*
  (see recipe on page 167)
- vegetable oil for frying

See step-by-step procedure on page 222

Traditionally, alcapurrias are shaped on a wilted wild grape leaf (uva playera), and slid from the leaf into the hot oil one by one. I provide a nontraditional method that eases the process for home cooks. If you would like to prepare them ahead of time, arrange them in rows on a sheet pan lined with parchment paper. Cover with plastic wrap, and freeze for a couple of hours before frying so they retain their shape.

Procedure:

1 Peel the *yautías*, remove any soft or blemished spots, and cut into pieces.

2 Place the peeled *yautías* in a food processor and finely grind, scraping the sides of the food processor with a rubber spatula from time to time. Pour in the *achiote* oil, add the *adobo*, and process to a smooth purée, about 5 minutes. The processed purée should be slimy and wet, free of lumps, and the bright yellow color of a cooked egg yolk. Refrigerate for about 20 minutes.

3 In a frying pan, or a deep fryer, heat about 3 inches of vegetable oil to 350°F.

4 Prepare the *alcapurrias*: Dip an oval ice cream scoop in water, and lightly pack it with the *yautía* purée. Dip your forefinger in olive oil, and press into the center of the purée to make a cavity, without reaching all the way in. Rotate your finger inside to widen the cavity (some of the *yautía* purée should slightly overflow). Add ½-teaspoon of *picadillo* to the cavity, and fold the overflowing *yautía* purée over it to seal. Using wet fingers, smooth out the surface so that no meat is showing and the filling is well enclosed.

5 Carefully slide the *alcapurria* from the scoop into the hot oil and deep fry for 4 to 5 minutes, or until golden brown. Repeat with the remaining *yautía* purée and *picadillo*. Using a slotted spoon, remove the *alcapurrias* from the oil, and set aside to drain on paper towels. Serve immediately.

átano yuca **viandas papa** relle
res tostones arañitas **amarillos**
yuca **viandas papa** piñón **pi**
platanutres tostones **arañitas** a
átano yuca **viandas papa** relle
res tostones arañitas **amarillos**
yuca **viandas papa** piñón **pi**
platanutres tostones **arañitas** a
átano yuca **viandas papa** relle
res tostones arañitas **amarillos**
yuca **viandas papa** piñón **pi**
platanutres tostones **arañitas** a

Chapter III

Plantains and roots

Plantains & Roots

The versatility of plantains & roots rivals that of the potato. They can be prepared in so many ways; it would take an entire book to talk about all the recipes and cooking applications that they can be subject to.

If I had to narrow down food categories to the most important one for Puerto Rico, I would certainly choose plantains and roots, since they are represented in every segment of our diet. They are the foundation for some of our most distinguished fritters, soups, *pasteles*, desserts, stews and fish recipes.

They provide comfort when we are sick, when we consume them mashed. They are the countryman's *(jíbaro)* power food when working in the agricultural fields. In the reinvention of our gastronomy they played a crucial role as chips, which were and are used as elements of crunch and providers of height in redesigning the look of our plates. They are important, as well, to the trend of setting proteins over mashed roots.

Some are even classified as roots, even if by scientific means they do not qualify as such. I am talking about *panas* or breadfruits, which grow on trees but, for purposes of everyday talk, are referred to as *viandas*, which is our way of generally categorizing root vegetables.

Yuca, or cassava as it is more commonly known internationally, was not only the foundation for the earliest form of bread that the *Taíno* Indians produced in Puerto Rico (which they called cassava as well), but also a source of starch for ironing in the old days.

Finally, in the local lingo when a person's facial structure clearly shows stereotypical features, we say they have *la mancha de plátano* or, literally translated, the plantain stain, which is the fundamental reason why I chose to present myself on the cover with a *racimo* of green plantains.

> **Chapter III**
>
> Plantains and roots

Platanutres

Plantain Chips

Makes about 5 dozen

Ingredients:

- 1 green plantain
- vegetable oil for frying
- salt for sprinkling

Procedure:

1 Peel the plantains: Cut off ½ inch from both ends of the plantains. Using a sharp knife, score the plantain's skin lengthwise in three different sections. Slide the tip of the knife or your finger under the skin and begin pulling away, going from top to bottom. (Doing this under running warm water facilitates the peeling and prevents your hands from getting stained and sticky.)

2 Cut the plantain into 4 equal parts with flat ends. Using a mandolin, slice each piece of plantain into round thin slices the thickness of a quarter or less. Dip the plantain chips in salted water briefly (no more than a couple of minutes) as you slice them, to prevent their natural starches from making them stick to each other.

3 In a frying pan or deep fryer, heat about 3 inches of vegetable oil to 350° F. Remove the plantain chips from the water and shake off any excess. Drop the chips into the hot oil in batches, stirring as they hit the oil so that they do not stick together while frying. Fry for about 3 minutes or until golden and crisp. Remove from the oil, and drain on paper towels. Sprinkle with salt (or garlic powder if you feel like getting a kick), and serve immediately. If stored in a tightly sealed jar or bag, *platanutres* will keep for about 2 days.

Platanutres are the Puerto Rican alternative to potato chips. They're great to snack on or as an accompaniment to sandwiches and other grab-and-go dishes.

Chapter III

Plantains and roots

Tostones de Plátano

Plantain "Tostones"

Makes about 32

Ingredients:

- 4 green plantains
- vegetable oil for frying
- salt for sprinkling

See step-by-step procedure on page 230

Procedure:

1 Peel the plantains: Cut off ½ inch from both ends of the plantains. Using a sharp knife, score the skin lengthwise in three different sections. Slide the tip of the knife or your finger under the skin and begin to pull it away, going from top to bottom. (Doing this under running warm water facilitates the peeling, and prevents your hands from getting stained and sticky.)

2 In a frying pan or deep fryer, heat about 2 inches of vegetable oil to 350° F. Cut the plantain into 1-inch pieces (or ½-inch for smaller *tostones*), and add to the hot oil. Fry for about 6 minutes until they start turning golden and are tender inside. Remove from the oil, and drain on paper towels. Using a mallet or the bottom of a tin can or a sauté pan, smash the plantains into ⅛-inch-thick *tostones*. If they stick to the pounding device, release them by quickly sliding a sharp knife under the *tostones*.

3 Quickly dip the *tostones* into a bowl of salted water. (If they are left to soak in the water too long, the *tostones* will turn soggy and disintegrate slowly.) Remove from the water, shake excess water off, and carefully return the *tostones* to the hot oil. Refry for another 5 minutes until they begin to turn golden. Remove from the oil, and drain on paper towels. Sprinkle with salt, and serve immediately.

The thickness of the tostones themselves will determine their crunchiness. Play around with different widths; my personal favorite is a tostón that's thin and crispy, yet maintains a soft, fleshy inside.

> **Chapter III**
>
> Plantains and roots

Tostones de Pana

Breadfruit *"Tostones"*
Makes about 4 dozen

Ingredients:

- 1 medium breadfruit
- vegetable oil for frying
- salt for sprinkling

Procedure:

1 Peel the breadfruit: Using a large knife, cut off the ends of the breadfruit. Stand it on its base, and cut off the rind from the sides using wide, downward strokes.

2 Cut the breadfruit lengthwise into quarters. Cut away the soft, spotted core as well as any blemishes (the flesh should be white and starchy like a potato), then slice the quarters into 1/2-inch thick wedges.

3 In a frying pan, heat about 2 inches of vegetable oil to 350°F. Add the wedges of breadfruit to the hot oil, and fry, in batches, until tender inside, about 7 minutes.

4 Remove the wedges from the oil, and drain on paper towels. Using a mallet, or the bottom of a large tin can or of a sauté pan, smash the breadfruit wedges into 1/4-inch thick *tostones*. If they stick to the pounding device, release them by quickly sliding a sharp knife under the *tostones*.

5 Return the *tostones* to the hot oil, and refry for another 5 minutes until they begin to turn golden. Remove from the oil, and drain on paper towels. Sprinkle with salt, and serve.

A certain amount of failure is expected in this recipe. The ripeness of the breadfruit determines the texture of the tostones; the breadfruit should be firm, not too ripe that the tostones will be sweet, or too green that they won't flatten. The thickness of the wedges and of the tostones themselves will determine their crunchiness, as well. Play around with different widths; my personal favorite is a tostón that's thin and crispy, yet maintains a soft, fleshy inside.

> **Chapter III**
>
> Plantains and roots

Arañitas

Plantain "Spiders"
Makes about 16

Ingredients:

- 2 medium green plantains
- vegetable oil for frying
- salt for sprinkling

See step-by-step procedure on page 228

Procedure:

1 Peel the plantains: Cut off ½ inch from both ends of the plantains. Using a sharp knife, score the skin lengthwise in three different sections. Slide the tip of the knife or your finger under the skin and begin to pull it away, going from top to bottom. (Doing this under running warm water facilitates the peeling.)

2 Grate the plantains through the medium holes of a grater to obtain thin shreds, and set aside.

3 In a frying pan, heat about 2 inches of vegetable oil to 350º F. With your hands, form loose bundles of 2 tablespoons of shredded plantain, applying light pressure to help the natural starches act as a glue to keep the shreds together. Drop the bundles, in batches, into the hot oil, leaving enough space between the bundles so they don't stick to each other. Fry for about 2 minutes or until golden and crisp. (There will be loose shreds of plantain escaping the bundles and floating freely on the oil.) In order to keep the oil clean, remove the loose shreds before adding the next batch of *arañitas*. Remove the *arañitas* from the oil, and drain on paper towels. Sprinkle with salt, and serve immediately.

Chapter III

Plantains and roots

Amarillos en Almíbar

Sweet Plantains in Syrup
Serves 4

Ingredients:
- 4 ripe plantains, peeled
- 2 tablespoons unsalted butter
- ½ teaspoon kosher salt
- ¾ cup sugar, divided
- 5 Goya cloves
- 2 Goya sticks cinnamon
- 2 pods star anise
- ½ cup dark Puerto Rican rum
- ¾ cups water

Procedure:

1 Slice the plantains in half crosswise. In a large skillet over medium-high heat, melt the butter sprinkled with the salt to speed up the browning process. Add the plantains, and brown for about 2 minutes on each side.

2 Sprinkle ¼ cup of sugar over the plantains, and add ¾ cup of water. Cook until the sugar starts to dissolve, about 2 minutes. Add the cloves, cinnamon and anise, and carefully deglaze the pan with the rum (remove the pan from the heat when adding the rum, for the flame can cause it to ignite). Add the remaining ½ cup of sugar, and stir. Cover, and cook over medium heat for about 10 minutes, until the plantains are soft and a syrupy sauce has formed. (Baste the plantains with the sauce throughout the cooking process.) Remove the lid, and cook for another 3 to 4 minutes.

Accommodating my very favorite flavor combination, this sweet preparation of starchy ripe plantains complements salty and cheesy dishes wonderfully. In Puerto Rico, an order of lasagna or spaghetti Bolognese is most probably followed by a side order of amarillos, *whether they be simply fried or steeped in* almíbar.

Chapter III

Plantains and roots

Mofongo de Amarillo

Ripe Plantain *"Mofongo"*

Makes about 6 servings

Ingredients:

- vegetable oil for frying
- 1 ripe plantain, peeled
- 2 green plantains, peeled
- 2 cloves garlic
- 4 slices cooked bacon
- 1 tablespoon Goya olive oil (not extra virgin)
- ¼ teaspoon salt

Procedure:

1 In a frying pan, heat about 2 inches of vegetable oil to 350° F. Cut the ripe plantain into ½-inch pieces and the green plantains into 1-inch pieces. Add the green plantains to the hot oil, and fry for about 5 minutes until golden on both sides and tender inside. Remove from the oil, and set aside to drain on paper towels.

2 Add the ripe plantain to the hot oil, and fry for about 2 minutes until golden on both sides. Remove from the oil, and set aside to drain on paper towels

3 In a food processor, finely grind the garlic. Add the bacon, and process until finely minced. Add the fried ripe and green plantains to the food processor, and grind. Scrape the side of the food processor with a rubber spatula, add the olive oil and the salt, and process the ingredients to a coarse paste. Form into medium size balls, and serve.

This version of mofongo, with its distinct combination of sweet and salty flavors, although non-traditional, makes a more refined accompaniment for meat and fish dishes. I especially recommend using it as stuffing for poultry and game.

Chapter III

Plantains and roots

Mofongo de Plátano

Green Plantain "*Mofongo*"

Makes 1 to 2 servings

Ingredients:

- 2 green plantains
- vegetable oil for frying
- 1 tablespoon Goya olive oil (not extra virgin)
- 2 cloves garlic
- ¼ teaspoon kosher salt
- ½ ounce pork cracklings (*chicharrón*), chopped
- 2 teaspoons chicken stock

Procedure:

1. Peel the plantains: Cut off ½ inch from both ends of the plantains. Using a sharp knife, score the skin lengthwise in three different sections. Slide the tip of the knife or your finger under the skin and begin to pull it away, going from top to bottom. (Doing this under running warm water facilitates the peeling.)

2. In a frying pan or deep fryer, heat about 2 inches of vegetable oil to 350° F. Cut the plantains into 1-inch pieces (or ½-inch for smaller *tostones*), and add to the hot oil. Fry for about 6 minutes until they start turning golden and are tender inside. Remove from the oil, and drain on paper towels.

3. Prepare the *mofongo:* Oil the inside of a wooden mortar with the olive oil. Add the garlic and ¼ teaspoon of salt and, with the pestle, pound the garlic to a paste. Add half of the fried plantains to the mortar and, with the pestle, pound to a coarse mash, incorporating the garlic paste as you pound. Add the pork cracklings, chicken stock and the remaining pieces of plantain. Season with ⅛ teaspoon of salt, and pound to mash the newly added plantains and incorporate the other ingredients. Rotate the mortar as you go, pounding with a downward motion towards the sides of the mortar (this helps to alternate the ingredients from the bottom of the mortar). Once the mixture is mashed, smooth out and flatten the surface. With the aid of a spoon, remove the *mofongo* from the mortar, and flip onto a plate. At this point the *mofongo* should look like a half dome.

A common way to serve *mofongo* is to dress it with fish or chicken stock, and eat it as a full meal. Nonetheless, stuffing the dome with stewed meat, chicken or shrimp has become widely popular in local restaurants.

Chapter III

Plantains and roots

Mofongo de Yuca

Cassava "*Mofongo*"
Makes 4 side dishes

Ingredients:

- 2½ pounds *yuca*
- vegetable oil for frying
- Goya olive oil (not extra virgin)
- kosher salt
- 2 cloves garlic
- 4 slices crisp bacon

Procedure:

1 Peel the *yuca*, cut into ½-inch thick pieces, and set aside.

2 In a frying pan or deep fryer, heat about 2 inches of vegetable oil to 350°F. Add the *yuca* to the hot oil, and fry, in batches, until golden and tender inside, about 6 minutes. Remove from the oil, and set aside to drain on paper towels.

3 Prepare the *mofongo*: Oil the inside of a wooden mortar with olive oil. Add 1 clove of garlic and ⅛ teaspoon of salt and, with the pestle, pound the garlic to a paste. Add ¼ of the fried *yuca* to the mortar and, with the pestle, pound to a coarse mash, incorporating the garlic paste as you pound. Finely chop 1 slice of bacon and add to the mortar. Pound to mash the *yuca* and incorporate the bacon. Rotate the mortar as you go, pounding with a downward motion towards the sides of the mortar (this helps to alternate the ingredients from the bottom of the mortar). Once the mixture is mashed, smooth out and flatten the surface. With the aid of a spoon, remove the *mofongo* from the mortar and flip it onto a plate. At this point the *mofongo* should look like a half dome.

4 Repeat with the remaining garlic, *yuca* and bacon to obtain 4 servings of *mofongo*.

Chapter III

Plantains and roots

Viandas Majadas

Mashed Root Vegetables
Serves 6 to 8

In contemporary Puerto Rican restaurants, it has become customary to serve proteins dressed with different flavor combinations over a bed of mashed root vegetables.

Ingredients:
- 12 ounces peeled and seeded *calabaza* (Caribbean Pumpkin)
- 12 ounces peeled *apio*, cubed
- 12 ounces peeled potato, cubed
- 12 ounces peeled *yautía*, cubed
- 6 tablespoons butter, cut into small pieces
- kosher salt

Procedure:

1 Place the root vegetables in a large stockpot. Add enough cold water to cover, and place over high heat. Bring to a boil, add ¼ cup of salt, and cook for about 30 minutes until the vegetables are fork-tender.

2 Drain the root vegetables, and transfer to a bowl. With a hand masher or a wire whisk, mash the roots to a soft yet lumpy consistency. (If you prefer a smooth purée, simply mash further.)

3 Add the butter, and stir until it melts into the mashed vegetables. Season with 1½ teaspoons of salt, and serve.

Mashed root vegetables possess that comforting quality we crave when we are feeling down or if it is cold and rainy outside. When I was growing up and came down with the flu, my grandmother Milagros would whip up some *viandas* for me. Their buttery warmth soothed the cold away.

Chapter III

Plantains and roots

Ensalada de Papa

Potato Salad

Serves 6 to 8

Ingredients:

- 3 pounds Idaho potatoes, peeled
- ¼ cup kosher salt
- 2 Red Delicious apples, peeled, cored and diced
- 2 stalks celery, fronds removed, peeled and diced
- 1 small onion, cut to a fine dice
- 1 cup shelled and cooked green peas
- ½ teaspoon salt
- ¼ teaspoon freshly ground white pepper
- 2 cups mayonnaise
- 4 hard-boiled eggs, shelled and coarsely chopped

Procedure:

1. Place the whole potatoes in a pot, and add enough water to cover. Add ¼ cup salt. Place over high heat and bring to a boil. Cook until fork-tender, 40-50 minutes. Drain the potatoes, and set aside to cool.

2. Cut the potatoes to a medium dice, and place in a bowl with the apples, celery, onion and peas. Season with ½ teaspoon of salt and the white pepper, and fold in the mayonnaise until well incorporated with the rest of the ingredients. Fold in the hard-boiled eggs.

3. Set aside in the refrigerator to chill for about 40 minutes before serving.

Chapter III

Plantains and roots

Piñón

Ripe Plantain and Beef Lasagna
Serves 6

Ingredients:

- vegetable oil for frying
- 6 ripe plantains, peeled
- 4 ounces steamed green beans, cut into pieces
- 4 cups *picadillo* (see recipe on page 167)
- 1 tablespoon Goya olive oil (not extra virgin)
- 6 eggs, beaten

Procedure:

1 Preheat the oven to 300°F. In a frying pan, heat about 2 inches of vegetable oil to 350°F. Slice the plantains lengthwise into quarters. Add to the hot oil, in batches, and fry for about 4 minutes until golden on both sides. Remove from the oil, and set aside to drain on paper towels.

2 In a bowl, combine the *picadillo* with the green beans, mix well, and set aside.

3 Prepare the *piñón*: Oil the bottom and sides of a 7" x 11" baking dish with the olive oil. Arrange a layer of the fried plantain slices on the bottom of the baking dish. (You may have to cut some plantain slices into smaller pieces to fill in any empty spaces). Press down with your hands. Add the *picadillo* mixture on top and spread into an even layer. Pour ¾ of the beaten eggs over the layer of meat, and prick the surface of the meat with a fork so that it absorbs the egg. (The egg holds the *piñón* together for even slicing). Arrange a layer of the remaining plantain slices on top (you may have to cut some plantain slices into smaller pieces to fill in any empty spaces). Pour the remaining eggs over the plantains, and with a rubber spatula spread into a thin layer.

4 Place the *piñón* in the oven, and bake for about 40 minutes, until the egg has cooked, the meat is heated through, and the surface of the *piñón* is golden and springy to the touch.

5 Remove the *piñón* from the oven, slice as you would a lasagna, and serve.

> Chapter III
>
> Plantains and roots

Piononos

Ripe Plantain and Beef Mold
Serves 6

Ingredients:

- vegetable oil for frying
- 6 ripe plantains, peeled
- Goya olive oil (not extra virgin) for greasing
- 4 cups *picadillo* (see recipe on page 167)
- 6 eggs, beaten

See step-by-step procedure on page 224

Procedure:

1 In a frying pan, heat about 2 inches of vegetable oil to 350° F. Slice the plantains into ¼-inch-thick rounds. Add to the hot oil, in batches, and fry for about 2 or 3 minutes until golden on both sides. Remove from the oil, and set aside to drain on paper towels.

2 Grease 6 ovenproof individual molds with olive oil, and line the bottoms with parchment paper. Line the molds with the plantain slices, pressing well against the sides of the molds. You may have to cut some plantain slices into smaller pieces to fit any empty spaces.

3 Preheat oven to 350° F. Distribute the *picadillo* among the plantain-lined molds. Pour the beaten eggs over the *piononos*. Bake until the eggs are set and the *piononos* are golden and springy to the touch.

4 When able to handle the *piononos*, but making sure they are still very hot, run a paring knife along the edges of the molds to help loosen the *piononos*. Turn upside down and tap, if necessary, to help them out. Make sure to discard the parchment paper.

Piononos are traditionally dipped in eggs and fried. I provide a lighter alternative to the island's staple road-stand treat.

Pasteles

"Yautía" and Pork Dumplings

Makes 8 *pasteles*

Ingredients:

- 1 pound pork butt
- 1 teaspoon *adobo* (see recipe on page 6)
- 2 tablespoons Goya olive oil (not extra virgin)
- 1 small onion, cut into small dice
- 4 cloves garlic, pounded to a paste
- ½ cubanelle pepper, seeds and inner white ribbing removed, cut into small dice
- 2 tablespoons *sofrito* (see recipe on page 13)
- 2 tablespoons chopped *culantro*
- ¼ cup Goya Spanish tomato sauce
- ½ cup Goya green olives stuffed with *pimientos*
- ½ cup canned Goya *garbanzo* beans (chickpeas), drained
- ½ cup raisins
- 5 cups *yautía masa*
- 8 plantain leaves, cut into 12"x12" squares

See step-by-step procedure on page 226

Procedure:

1 Clean the meat: Cut away and discard the excess fat from the pork butt. (There should be an almost equal ratio of fat to meat on the piece.) Cut the remaining meat into small dice, season with the *adobo*, and set aside.

2 In a sauté pan, warm the olive oil. Add the pork to the pan and brown, stirring occasionally, for about 3 minutes. Add the onion, garlic, cubanelle pepper, *sofrito* and *culantro*, stir, and cook for another 2 minutes until the onion is translucent and loses its raw taste.

3 Stir in the tomato sauce, olives, *garbanzos* and raisins, and stir in 1 cup of water. Reduce the heat to medium, and cook, stirring occasionally, until all the liquid is absorbed, the flavors have concentrated and the pork is very tender, about 30 minutes. Remove from the heat, and set aside to cool to room temperature.

4 Meanwhile, wilt the plantain leaves: Remove any tough stems from the borders of the plantain leaves. Using tongs, wilt them over an open gas flame or electric coil for about 20 seconds on each side, making sure there is continuous movement over the flame or they will burn. Wilting the leaves makes them more pliable and releases their natural oils to flavor the *pasteles*.

Continues on next page >

> Chapter III
>
> Plantains and roots

5 Assemble the *pasteles*: In a bowl, combine the *yautía masa* with the pork mixture and mix well. Place a plantain leaf on a flat surface. Place 1 cup of the pork-*masa* mixture on the center of the leaf, leaving at least 2 inches of space on the sides. Fold the lower edge of the leaf shape over the mixture and fold over again twice, as you would a parcel. With your hands, push the filling from the open sides towards the center, to tighten the parcel. Fold the open sides under the parcel to close, and set aside. Repeat with the remaining plantain leaves and the pork-*masa* mixture.

6 Place the *pasteles* in a bamboo steamer for about 20 minutes until the *masa* maintains its shape and has cooked through. To serve, remove the *pastel* from the plantain parcel. If your urge for authenticity is such, pair up the parcels, truss them with butcher's twine and freeze. To cook, simply arrange the *pasteles* in a pot. Cover with water, and boil for about 45 minutes.

Making pasteles the traditional way can be a labor intensive process. The *masa* needs to be laid on the plantain leaf, and all the stuffing ingredients added separately before wrapping and shaping the *pastel*. These would then be wrapped, in pairs, in parchment paper, trussed, and boiled for hours in a large pot of water. Freeing them of the twine and all the different wet wrapping layers can be chaotic and very well worth every minute spent but, quite frankly, unnecessary. Although many traditionalists might object to my method of making *pasteles*, I stand by the fact that it provides an easier and quicker alternative while preserving the true flavors of this quintessential dish.

Seafood, rabbit, forced meats and other foods can be made into stuffing for *pasteles*. If you would rather hold back on the meat, play around with vegetables and legumes.

lo sopa fideos asopao vianda
erenjena guingambó guisa
lla sancocho fricasé cabrito pa
lo sopa fideos asopao vianda
erenjena guingambó guisa
lla sancocho fricasé cabrito pa
lo sopa fideos asopao vianda
erenjena guingambó guisa
lla sancocho fricasé cabrito pa
lo sopa fideos asopao vianda
erenjena guingambó guisa
lla sancocho fricasé cabrito pa

Chapter IV

Soups and stews

Soups and Stews

In our culture, soup is one of those items that have some medicinal properties, at least according to my grandmother Milagros, who claims to have used soup to cure our colds as children. Some soups are considered effective in helping soften the affects of a hangover. Since a lot of drinking is done throughout the weekend, you will find a whole lot of down-home-style restaurants offering *Sancocho* (a hearty Beef and Root Vegetable Stew) every Monday on their menu, in an effort to help headaches and other related ailments go away.

Chicken Soup *(Sopa de Pollo)* is at the top of the list. It is served with noodles, thinner than those used elsewhere, which we call *tallarines*. The flavoring herbs are *cilantro* and oregano and the taste is simple yet so great.

The culture has been crazy about the use of MSG for decades, without knowing it. A great deal of the broth produced for soups at home was started with fresh chickens and a couple of chicken broth cubes filled with salt and MSG, that kicks everything up a notch: all in the name and pursuit of a stronger-tasting product in the end.

There are three principal categories of soup when it comes to the true traditions of our little island. First and foremost, are the broth-based soups such as the one described earlier, either in its chicken, beef or fish broth or *caldo* versions.

Second, and not necessarily having any order of importance for the locals, are root-based soups or potages, as the French would name them. One that stands out is *Sopa de Platano* or Plantain Soup. Then, there is *Calabaza* (Caribbean Pumpkin) Soup, made from a squash which will differ a bit from its mainland pumpkin variety in its shape and flavor. There is an array of traditional *potages*, ranging from single root recipes to combinations of several, or even a few of the starchy vegetables we call *viandas*. For instance, my favorite one is *Apio* which, if translated to English, would mean celery. However, this *apio* has more of a yellow color skin with even deeper-yellow meat inside, and less of a structured shape than celery root has. Of all the roots, it is the one that costs the most, yields the least and is the hardest to peel.

The third category of what composes the most frequently consumed soup-like dish, is *asopao*. It is a rice-based soup that can be made from chicken, fish, shrimp, crab and lobster, and it turns out to be a meal on its own, depending on the size of the bowl. It is accompanied with avocado slices, bread or buttered soda crackers.

Our gastronomy is one that is rustic and delicious, and soups are, without doubt, one of the most popular first courses in Puerto Rican menu construction.

Caldo de Pollo Criollo

Chicken Stock
Makes 4 quarts

Because chicken stock is used widely throughout this book, I chose to provide a recipe for a stock that concentrated the true flavors of *criollo* cooking with the addition of *culantro*, bay leaves and peppercorns. I recommend using this particular preparation whenever one of the book's recipes calls for chicken stock.

Ingredients:

- 1 whole chicken, about 4 pounds, innards removed (neck reserved)
- 2 onions, roughly chopped
- 3 stalks celery, roughly chopped
- 2 carrots, peeled and roughly chopped
- 2 heads garlic, cut in half crosswise
- 15 leaves *culantro*
- 10 Goya dried bay leaves
- 1 teaspoon black peppercorns

Procedure:

1 Separate the chicken into parts: With a knife, remove the wings and thighs from the chicken, and set aside. Cut out the chicken's neck and backbone entirely, and set aside. Split the breast in two, and cut each breast into 3 pieces.

2 Place the chicken in a large stockpot with the onion, celery, carrots, garlic, *culantro*, bay leaves and peppercorns. Pour in 8 quarts of cold water, and place over high heat. Bring to a full boil, and cook for about 30 minutes. Lower the heat, and simmer for another 2½ hours. If your taste buds require more intensity of flavor, simmer the stock an additional 1 to 1½ hours.

3 Remove from the heat, pour the stock into a large clean container, and set aside to cool at room temperature. Cover, and refrigerate overnight to facilitate the skimming process. After refrigeration the fat should form a solid layer on the surface of the stock. Skim off the layer of concentrated fat before using the stock.

The fat that is skimmed from the surface of the stock can be used as a butter or oil substitute. It provides a wonderful flavor to sautéed vegetables.

Chapter IV

Soups and stews

Caldo de Res

Beef Stock

Makes 4 quarts

Ingredients:

- 4 pounds cubed stewing beef, bone-in
- 2 onions, roughly chopped
- 3 stalks celery, roughly chopped
- 2 carrots, peeled and roughly chopped
- 2 heads garlic, cut in half crosswise
- 15 leaves *culantro*
- 10 Goya dried bay leaves
- 1 teaspoon black peppercorns

Procedure:

1. Place the beef in a large stockpot with the onion, celery, carrots, garlic, *culantro*, bay leaves and peppercorns. Pour in 8 quarts of cold water, and place over high heat. Bring to a full boil, and cook for about 1 hour. Lower the heat, and simmer for another 3 hours.

2. Remove from the heat, pour the stock into a large clean container, and set aside to cool at room temperature. Cover, and refrigerate overnight to facilitate the skimming process. After refrigeration the fat should form a solid layer on the surface of the stock. Skim off the layer of concentrated fat before using the stock.

PUERTO RICO TRUE FLAVORS

> Chapter IV
>
> Soups and stews

Caldo de Pescado

Fish Stock

Makes 4 quarts

Ingredients:

- 4¾ pounds fish bones
- 2 onions, roughly chopped
- 3 stalks celery, roughly chopped
- 2 carrots, peeled and roughly chopped
- 2 heads garlic, cut in half crosswise
- 15 leaves *culantro*
- 10 Goya dried bay leaves
- 1 teaspoon black peppercorns

Procedure:

1. Place the fish bones in a large stockpot with the onion, celery, carrots, garlic, *culantro*, bay leaves and peppercorns. Pour in 8 quarts of cold water, and place over high heat. Bring to a full boil, and cook for 30 minutes. Lower the heat, and simmer for another 30 to 45 minutes.

2. Remove from the heat, pour the stock into a large clean container, and set aside to cool at room temperature. Cover, and refrigerate overnight to facilitate the skimming process. After refrigeration the fat should form a solid layer on the surface of the stock. Skim off the layer of concentrated fat before using the stock.

> **Chapter IV**
>
> Soups and stews

Sopa de Pollo y Fideos

Chicken Noodle Soup
Serves 6

Ingredients:

- 2 quarts plus 1 cup chicken stock (see recipe on page 72)
- 3 tablespoons *sofrito* (see recipe on page 13)
- 2 Idaho potatoes, peeled and cut into large dice
- 2 skinless & boneless chicken breasts, cut into large dice
- 3 tablespoons chopped *cilantro*
- 4 ounces dry, thin noodles (*tallarines*)
- 1 tablespoon kosher salt

Procedure:

1. In a large saucepan over medium-high heat, combine the chicken stock with the *sofrito*, and bring to a full boil.

2. Add the potatoes, chicken breasts and *cilantro*, and simmer for 4 minutes. Break up the noodles, add to the soup, and cook for another 8 minutes. Season the soup with the salt, stir, and remove from the heat. Serve while piping hot. (If left to cool, the noodles will soak up a lot of the liquid, resulting in a broth-less soup).

An efficient cure for the common cold, homemade chicken noodle soup, as in just about any other culture, is the home remedy of choice in many Puerto Rican households. The presence of sofrito and cilantro gives it that distinct island flavor.

Asopao de Pollo

Chicken and Rice Soup

Serves 6

Chapter IV

Soups and stews

Asopao de *Pollo* is a staple of Puerto Rican cuisine. There are variations of the chicken and rice stew from household to household. Most *asopaos* are prepared with a butchered whole chicken. In an attempt to save you the somewhat torturous task of removing small chicken bones from your bowl (as I did on my early encounters with my *Tía Tati's* delicious *asopao*), I chose to use boneless chicken thighs.

In my mother's house, *asopao* was usually accompanied with Export Soda Crackers spread with softened butter.

Ingredients:

- 1 pound boneless skinless chicken thighs, cubed
- 3 teaspoons *adobo* (see recipe on page 6)
- 3 teaspoons *achiote* oil (see recipe on page 6)
- 1 garlic clove, pounded to a paste
- 3 tablespoons *sofrito* (see recipe on page 13)
- 4 tablespoons chopped *culantro*, divided
- 1 cup Goya Spanish tomato sauce
- ½ cup short-grain rice
- 2 quarts chicken stock (see recipe on page 72)
- 3 teaspoons Goya capers

Procedure:

1 Season the chicken with the *adobo*, and set aside in the refrigerator to marinate for at least 1 hour. If time allows, marinate overnight.

2 In a *caldero*, over medium-high heat, warm the *achiote* oil. Add the chicken to the saucepan along with the garlic, *sofrito*, 1 tablespoon of *culantro* and the tomato sauce. Add the rice, and cook for about 2 minutes, stirring to make sure the rice is well coated with the fat and the tomato sauce.

3 Pour in the chicken stock, stirring to scrape any browned bits from the bottom of the pan, and bring to a boil. Lower the heat, and simmer for 5 minutes. Stir in the capers, and cook for another 25 minutes until the liquid has reduced and the rice and chicken are cooked. (Make sure to skim off the impurities that rise to the surface of the *asopao* during the simmering. This step will provide for a cleaner product with a greater concentration of flavor). Stir in the remaining 2 tablespoons of *culantro*, and serve hot with a side of *tostones* (see recipe on page 47).

When first approaching this recipe, the amount of rice might seem small in ratio to the liquid. Because rice grains are porous, they absorb great amounts of liquid while cooking, reducing the initial amounts of liquid in the recipe. Trust me on this, and stick to the amount of rice suggested.

> **Chapter IV**
>
> Soups and stews

Sopa de Viandas

Root Vegetable Soup

Serves 6 to 8

Ingredients:

- 3 tablespoons Goya olive oil (not extra virgin)
- ⅔ cup of *sofrito* (see recipe on page 13)
- 3 leaves *culantro*, chopped
- 3 quarts chicken stock (see recipe on page 72)
- 6 ounces peeled *apio*, cubed
- 6 ounces peeled potato, cubed
- ⅛ cup white vinegar
- 6 ounces peeled *yautía lila*, cubed
- 6 ounces peeled *yautía blanca*, cubed
- 6 ounces peeled and seeded *calabaza* (Caribbean Pumpkin), cubed
- 6 ounces peeled *ñame*, cubed
- 3 teaspoons kosher salt
- 2 tablespoons chopped *cilantro*

Procedure:

1 In a large saucepan over medium-high heat, warm the olive oil. Add the *sofrito* and *culantro*, and cook for about 1 minute until the ingredients have lost their raw taste.

2 Pour in the chicken stock, and stir, scraping any browned bits from the bottom of the pan. Add the root vegetables, and bring to a full boil. Cover, lower the heat, and simmer for about 25 minutes until the vegetables are fork-tender.

3 Pour the soup into a blender and process to a smooth purée, thick enough to coat the back of a spoon. If using an immersion blender, submerge the entire blade into the soup and purée to the suggested consistency. If you prefer a thinner consistency, feel free to add some chicken stock as you purée the soup.

4 Season with 3 teaspoons of salt, and stir in the chopped *cilantro*. If you want a richer flavor or a shinier look to the pureed soup, stir in 4 ounces of whole butter. Serve hot.

> Chapter IV
>
> Soups and stews

Sopa de Plátano

Plantain Soup

Serves 8

Ingredients:

- 4 green plantains, peeled
- 3 tablespoons Goya olive oil (not extra virgin)
- 3 tablespoons *sofrito* (see recipe on page 13)
- 3 garlic cloves, pounded to a paste
- 2 quarts plus 1 cup chicken stock (see recipe on page 72)
- 1 tablespoon kosher salt
- 2 tablespoons chopped *cilantro*

Procedure:

1. Grate the plantains through the medium holes of a grater to obtain thin shreds. Cover so they don't oxidize, and set aside.

2. In a large saucepan or stockpot over medium-high heat, warm the olive oil. Add the *sofrito* and garlic. Cook, stirring, for about 2 minutes until the ingredients have lost their raw taste but no browning has occurred. Pour in the chicken stock, stir, and bring to a full boil. Add the plantains, and stir.

3. Lower the heat, and simmer for about 25 minutes, stirring from time to time to prevent the starchy plantains from sticking to the bottom of the pan.

4. Pour the soup into a blender and process to a smooth purée, thick enough to coat the back of a spoon. If using an immersion blender, submerge the entire blade into the soup and purée to the suggested consistency. If you prefer a thinner consistency, feel free to add some chicken stock as you purée the soup.

5. Season with 1 tablespoon of salt, stir in the chopped *cilantro*, and serve.

To provide a texture contrast to this rich soup, sprinkle some crumbled *arañitas* (see recipe on page 51) over the plated soup.

Chapter IV

Soups and stews

Caribbean Pumpkin Soup
Serves 12

Sopa de Calabaza

Ingredients:

- 3 tablespoons Goya olive oil (not extra virgin)
- ½ cup *sofrito* (see recipe on page 13)
- 1 large onion, chopped
- 4 pounds *calabaza* (Caribbean Pumpkin) or substitute pumpkin, peeled and seeds removed, cubed
- ½ cup sugar
- 2 quarts plus 1 cup chicken stock (see recipe on page 72)
- 1 tablespoon kosher salt

Procedure:

1 In a stockpot over medium-high heat, warm the olive oil. Add the *sofrito* and the onion. Cook, stirring until the onion is translucent and loses its raw taste.

2 Add the *calabaza* and the sugar, and stir to coat well. Pour in the chicken stock, and bring to a boil. Cover, lower the heat, and simmer for about 25 minutes. Remove the lid, and cook for another 10 to 15 minutes until the liquid reduces by one third.

3 Pour the soup into a blender and process to a smooth purée, thick enough to coat the back of a spoon. If using an immersion blender, submerge the entire blade into the soup and purée to the suggested consistency. If you prefer a thinner consistency, feel free to add some chicken stock as you purée the soup. Correct the seasoning with kosher salt if necessary.

This simple soup can be dressed up with a variation of garnishes. Sprinkle roasted *pepitas* (pumpkin seeds) or toasted sesame seeds on top, or drizzle some *cilantro* or basil pesto over the plated soup. For those with a sweet tooth, drizzle some maple syrup in the center of the plated soup, and finish with a dash of chopped chives.

> Chapter IV
>
> Soups and stews

Berenjena Guisada

Stewed Eggplant

Serves 6

Ingredients:

- ⅓ cup Goya olive oil (not extra virgin)
- ½ cup *sofrito* (see recipe on page 13)
- 1 onion, diced
- 1 cubanelle pepper, seeds and inner white ribbings removed, diced
- 4 cloves garlic, mashed down to a paste
- 1 tablespoon salt
- 3 cups Goya Spanish tomato sauce
- 4 pounds eggplant, peeled and cut into cubes
- ⅓ cup chopped *culantro*

Procedure:

1 In a large sauté pan, warm the olive oil. Add the *sofrito*, onion, pepper and garlic, and season with 1 teaspoon of salt. Stir, and cook for about 4 minutes until the onion is translucent and has lost its raw taste.

2 Add the tomato sauce, and cook for about 2 minutes, stirring. Add the eggplant; pour in 2 cups of water, and season with 1 tablespoon of salt. Stir well, and bring to a boil. Reduce the heat to medium, cover, and simmer for about 45 minutes until the eggplant is soft and has absorbed some of the sauce. Stir in the *culantro*, and remove from the heat. Serve hot with a side of white rice or over pasta for a unique vegetarian dish.

Stewed eggplant and salt cod marry beautifully. For a heartier stew, stir 1 pound of pre-soaked salt cod in with the eggplant, as instructed in step 2.

Chapter IV

Soups and stews

Guingambó Guisado

Stewed Okra

Serves 6

Ingredients:

- 3 tablespoons Goya olive oil (not extra virgin)
- 1 onion, diced
- 1 cubanelle pepper, seeds and inner white ribbing removed, diced
- 4 cloves garlic, mashed down to a paste
- ⅓ cup *sofrito* (see recipe on page 13)
- 1 pound fresh okra, cut into ½-inch thick pieces
- 1 ¾ cups Goya Spanish tomato sauce
- ⅓ cup Goya green olives stuffed with *pimientos*
- 5 tablespoons chopped *culantro*, divided
- 1 tablespoon kosher salt

Procedure:

1. In a sauté pan over medium-high heat, warm the olive oil. Add the onion, garlic, pepper and *sofrito* and cook for about 3 minutes, until the onion is translucent and the vegetables have lost their raw taste.

2. Add the tomato sauce, stir, and cook for 2 minutes. Add the okra, olives, and 3 tablespoons of *culantro*. Stir in 2 cups of water, season with the salt, and bring to a slow simmer. Cover, and cook for about 40 minutes, stirring occasionally, until the okra is tender and the sauce has thickened. Remove from the heat, and serve over rice or with a side of *tostones*.

Guingambó journeyed our way through the African slave population and found its way into local dishes such as this stew. Okra produces a slightly slimy by-product when cooked; which might justify its dwindling popularity.

When picking the okra for this or any other okra dish, pick the youngest and smallest to avoid any possibility of the okra having a woody texture.

> Chapter IV
>
> Soups and stews

Corned Beef

Makes 4 cups

Ingredients:

- 3 tablespoons Goya olive oil (not extra virgin)
- 3 tablespoons *sofrito* (see recipe on page 13)
- 2 tablespoons chopped *culantro*
- 1 large onion, cut into small dice
- 1 cubanelle pepper, seeds and inner white ribbing removed, cut into small dice
- 2 cups Goya Spanish tomato sauce
- ½ cup chicken stock
- 1¾ pounds pre-cooked ground corned beef brisket

Procedure:

1 In a large sauté pan over medium-high heat, warm the olive oil. Add the *sofrito*, *culantro*, the onion and the pepper. Cook, stirring until the onion is translucent and loses its raw taste, about 3 minutes.

2 Add the tomato sauce, the corned beef and chicken stock, and stir until all the ingredients are well incorporated. Lower the heat and cook, stirring occasionally, until the stew has reduced, the red color has intensified, and the flavors have concentrated, about 25 minutes. A scattered occasional bubbling should occur during cooking, indicating that the moisture is being drawn away from the stew to achieve a tight yet moist texture.

A typical lunch staple, Corned Beef is usually served accompanied with white rice. Stirring 6 ounces of cubed fried ripe plantains, French fries or cooked string beans into the stew is customary, enhancing its flavor and texture. Corned Beef is also delicious paired with a fried egg or stirred into scrambled eggs. To demonstrate the dish's versatility, while testing this recipe we simply grabbed a bun and made ourselves a Puerto Rican version of a Sloppy Joe.

Corned Beef *Burritos* are a staple at Payá (www.payapr.com), my casual dining restaurant.

> Chapter IV
>
> Soups and stews

Jamonilla Guisada

Stewed Luncheon Meat

Serves 6

Luncheon meat is a perfect example of how a non-indigenous product makes it to another culture's gastronomic mainstream. If you are not a local, you might not be aware of the luncheon meat's strong culinary influence but, for me, growing up in our school system's cafeterias, fried and stewed luncheon meat, as well as luncheon meat rice, was always something to look forward to. If you develop an addiction to luncheon meat after trying this recipe, please do not hold me accountable.

Ingredients:

- 2 tablespoons Goya olive oil (not extra virgin)
- 3 12-ounce cans luncheon meat, cut into large dice
- 4 garlic cloves, mashed down to a paste
- 1 onion, cut into large dice
- 1 cubanelle pepper, seeds and inner white ribbing removed, cut into large dice
- ½ cup white vinegar
- 3 cups Goya Spanish tomato sauce
- 2 Idaho potatoes, peeled and cut into ½-inch cubes
- ½ cup Goya green olives
- 2 tablespoon Goya capers
- 2 teaspoons salt
- ¼ cup sugar
- 5 tablespoons chopped *culantro*, divided
- 1 cup shelled green peas (or substitute sweet corn kernels)

Procedure:

1 Add the olive oil to a large sauté pan over medium-high heat so it thinly coats the bottom. Add the luncheon meat, and cook for about 6 minutes, turning occasionally until browned on all sides.

2 Add the garlic, onion and pepper, and cook for about 5 minutes until the onion is translucent, stirring occasionally and scraping the bottom of the pan so that no scorching occurs. Stir in the vinegar, tomato sauce, potatoes, olives, capers and 1 quart of water. Season with the salt and sugar, and add 2 tablespoons of *culantro*. Stir, and bring to a simmer. Cook for about 20 minutes until the flavors are developed and the sauce has thickened, stirring occasionally and skimming off the impurities and fat that concentrates on the surface of the stew.

3 Stir in the green peas and the remaining 3 tablespoons of *culantro*, and cook for another 5 minutes. Remove from the heat, and serve over white rice.

Chapter IV

Soups and stews

Sancocho

Root Vegetable and Beef Stew

Serves 6

Ingredients:

- 2 pounds beef top round, cut into ½-inch cubes
- ¼ cup Goya olive oil (not extra virgin)
- 2 teaspoons *adobo* (see recipe on page 6)
- 3 tablespoons *sofrito* (see recipe on page 13)
- 1 large onion, cut into small dice
- 2 garlic cloves, pounded to a paste
- 1 small carrot, peeled and cut into small dice
- 2 stalks celery, cut into small dice
- 2 teaspoons kosher salt
- 1½ cups Goya Spanish tomato sauce
- 2 quarts chicken stock (see recipe on page 72)
- 8 ounces *yautía*, peeled and cut into ½-inch cubes
- 8 ounces potato, peeled and cut into ½-inch cubes
- 1 green plantain, peeled and cut into ½-inch cubes
- 2 tablespoons chopped *cilantro*
- 1 ear of corn, cut into 8 parts

Procedure:

1 Season the meat with the *adobo*, and set aside. In a large heavy bottomed pot over medium-high heat, warm the olive oil until it starts to smoke. Add the meat and sear for about 3 minutes on each side.

2 Add the *sofrito*, onion, garlic, carrot and celery. Season with 2 teaspoons of salt and cook, stirring, for 3 minutes until the onion loses its raw taste. Add the tomato sauce, and cook for another 4 minutes, stirring occasionally so that no scorching occurs. At this point the mixture should look like a thick meat stew.

3 Add the chicken stock, and bring to a full boil. Add the *yautía*, potato, plantain and corn, and return to a full boil. Cover, lower the heat, and simmer for 35 to 40 minutes until the vegetables are fork-tender and the meat is very soft.

4 Remove the *sancocho* from the heat, and stir in the chopped *cilantro*. Serve hot on its own or with a side of white rice or *tostones* (see recipe on page 47).

Like any other one-pot dish, Sancocho surely satisfies the hungry, combining protein, starches and veggies in one bowl. So great are its powers, that it is said to cure the worst of hangovers, or simply provide a drinker that second wind necessary to continue a long night of celebration.

Chapter IV

Soups and stews

Fricasé de Pollo

Chicken Stew

Serves 8

Ingredients:

- 1 whole chicken, about 4 pounds
- 1 tablespoon *adobo* (see recipe on page 6)
- 2 tablespoons white vinegar
- 3 tablespoons *achiote* oil (see recipe on page 6)
- ⅔ cup of *sofrito* (see recipe on page 13)
- 1 onion, diced
- 4 cloves garlic, pounded to a paste
- 1 cubanelle pepper, seeds and inner white ribbing removed, diced
- 3 tablespoons chopped *culantro*
- 3 cups dry cooking sherry
- 1¾ cups Goya Spanish tomato sauce
- 2 Idaho potatoes, peeled and cut into ½-inch cubes
- 2 carrots, peeled and cut into ½-inch thick pieces
- ½ cup Goya green olives stuffed with *pimientos*
- ¼ cup Goya capers
- 3 Goya bay leaves
- 1 tablespoon kosher salt

Procedure:

1 Separate the chicken into parts: With a knife, remove the wings, thighs and drumsticks from the chicken, and set aside. Cut out the chicken's backbone entirely (discard or reserve for chicken stock if desired). Split the breast in two, and set aside. With a cleaver, split each breast in half lengthwise, and cut each piece into 4 even-sized pieces, careful to keep the skin as intact as possible. Set aside. Cut and discard the joint bone from the drumsticks, cut the drumsticks in two, and set aside. Remove the central bone from the thighs, and cut each thigh into 6 parts, be careful to keep the skin intact.

2 In a bowl, combine the chicken with the *adobo* and vinegar. Stir well to coat, and set aside in the refrigerator to marinate for at least 1 hour. If time allows, marinate overnight.

3 In a large saucepan over medium-high heat, warm the *achiote* oil. Add the chicken, and brown for about 6 minutes on all sides. Add the *sofrito*, onion, garlic, pepper and *culantro*, and cook, stirring, for about 5 minutes.

4 Deglaze the pan with the wine, and cook until it starts to evaporate, about 4 minutes. Stir in the tomato sauce, and add the potatoes, carrots, olives and capers. Pour in 1½ quarts of water, add the bay leaves, and season with 1 tablespoon of salt. Bring to a full boil, and cook for about 10 minutes.

5 Reduce the heat, cover, and simmer for about 1 hour, stirring occasionally and skimming the surface of the stew. Once finished, the chicken should be tender enough to fall off the bone, and the sauce thick enough to coat the back of a spoon. Remove from the heat.

6 Remove and discard the bay leaves before serving. Serve piping hot with a side of white rice.

Fricasé de Ternera

Veal Stew
Serves 6 to 8

Ingredients:

- 2½ pounds stewing veal, cut into 1-inch cubes
- 1 tablespoon *adobo* (see recipe on page 6)
- 2 teaspoons chopped *culantro*
- 1 tablespoon white vinegar
- 4 tablespoons Goya olive oil (not extra virgin), divided
- ⅔ cup of *sofrito* (see recipe on page 13)
- 1 onion, cut into large dice
- 8 cloves garlic, minced
- 1 cubanelle pepper, seeds and inner white ribbing removed, cut into large dice
- 2 carrots, peeled, cut into 1-inch thick pieces
- 2 cups dry cooking sherry
- 1 cup Goya Spanish tomato sauce
- 2 Idaho potatoes, peeled and cut into 1-inch cubes
- ½ cup Goya green olives
- 2 tablespoons Goya capers
- ½ teaspoon black peppercorns
- 5 Goya dried bay leaves
- 3 tablespoons chopped oregano (or substitute 1 tablespoon Goya dried)
- 1 tablespoon salt

Procedure:

1 In a bowl, combine the veal with the *adobo*, *culantro*, vinegar and 1 tablespoon of olive oil. Stir well to coat, and set aside in the refrigerator to marinate for at least 1 hour. If time allows, marinate overnight.

2 In a large saucepan over medium-high heat, warm 3 tablespoons olive oil until it starts to smoke. Add the veal, and brown for about 6 minutes on all sides. Add the *sofrito*, onion, garlic, pepper and carrots and cook, stirring, for about 5 minutes.

3 Deglaze the pan with the wine, and cook until it starts to evaporate, about 4 minutes. Stir in the tomato sauce, and add the potatoes, olives and capers. Pour in 2 quarts of water; add the peppercorns, bay leaves and oregano, and season with 1 tablespoon of salt. Bring to a boil, and cook for about 10 minutes.

4 Reduce the heat, cover, and simmer for about 2 hours, stirring occasionally and skimming the surface of the stew. Once finished, the veal should be tender and moist, and the sauce thick enough to coat the back of a spoon. Remove from the heat.

5 Remove and discard the bay leaves before serving. Serve piping hot with a side of white rice.

Chapter IV

Soups and stews

Fricasé de Cabrito

Stewed Goat

Serves 6 to 8

Although it might seem a bit extraordinary, stewing goat meat with grape juice is quite common in the countryside. Back in the old days, the availability, or perhaps the high price, of wine led to more creative ways of tenderizing meat while stewing. The grape juice actually gives the stew a pleasant fruity layer of flavor.

Ingredients:

- 4½ pounds stewing goat meat, cut into 1-inch pieces (some pieces may have bones)
- 2 teaspoons *adobo* (see recipe on page 6)
- 2 tablespoons vinegar
- 1 cup *sofrito* (see recipe on page 13), divided
- ½ cup Goya olive oil (not extra virgin)
- 2 onions, cubed
- 8 cloves garlic, mashed down to a paste
- 1 cubanelle pepper, seeds and inner white ribbing removed, cubed
- 2 carrots, peeled and cut into 1-inch pieces
- 2 cups dry cooking sherry
- 1 ¾ cups Goya Spanish tomato sauce
- 2 Idaho potatoes, peeled and cut into 1-inch cubes
- ½ cup Goya green olives stuffed with *pimientos*
- 1 cup raisins
- 2 quarts grape juice
- 4 tablespoons chopped *culantro*
- 5 Goya dried bay leaves
- 2 tablespoons black peppercorns
- salt

Procedure:

1 In a bowl, combine the goat meat with the *adobo*, vinegar and ⅓ cup of *sofrito*. Stir well to coat and set aside in the refrigerator to marinate for at least 1 hour. If time allows, marinate overnight.

2 In a large heavy-bottomed pot over medium-high heat, warm the olive oil. Add the onion, garlic, pepper, the remaining ⅔ cup of *sofrito* and the carrots. Cook, stirring occasionally, until the onion is translucent and has lost its raw taste, about 5 minutes.

3 Deglaze the pan with the wine, cook until it starts to evaporate, about 4 minutes. Stir in the tomato sauce, the goat meat, potatoes, olives and raisins. Pour in the grape juice, and add the *culantro*, bay leaves and peppercorns. Pour in 3 quarts of water, season with 1 tablespoon of salt, and bring to a full boil.

4 Lower the heat, and cook for about 2 hours and 20 minutes on a rolling simmer, stirring occasionally so that the starchy ingredients do not settle on the bottom and cause scorching. At this point the meat should be tender enough to fall off the bone. Raise the heat, and cook for an additional 30 minutes until the sauce thickens enough to coat the back of a spoon. Remove from the heat.

5 Remove and discard the bay leaves and serve the stew with a side of white rice or *tostones de pana* (see recipe on page 49).

> **Chapter IV**
>
> Soups and stews

Carne Guisada

Beef Stew

Serves 4 to 6

Ingredients:

- 4 pounds beef (preferably top round), cut into 1-inch cubes (some pieces may have bones)
- 2 teaspoons *adobo* (see recipe on page 6)
- 2 tablespoons Goya olive oil (not extra virgin)
- 4 cloves garlic, minced
- ½ onion, cubed
- ½ cup *sofrito* (see recipe on page 13)
- 1 cup Goya Spanish tomato sauce
- 3 tablespoons chopped *culantro*
- 2 Idaho potatoes, peeled and cut into cubes
- 1 large carrot, peeled and sliced into ½-inch pieces
- 2 teaspoons salt
- ½ cup Goya green olives stuffed with *pimientos*

Procedure:

1 Season the meat with the *adobo*, and set aside. In a large saucepan or stockpot over high heat, warm the olive oil. Add the meat, and brown for about 3 minutes on each side without stirring excessively so that proper caramelization occurs.

2 Add the garlic and onion, and cook for about 3 minutes until the onion is translucent and has lost its raw taste. Stir in the *sofrito*, tomato sauce and *culantro*, and cook for about 2 minutes. Add the potatoes and carrot, and stir well to coat with the sauce. Pour in 2 quarts of water, season with 2 teaspoons of salt, and bring to a full boil.

3 Reduce the heat to medium, and simmer for about 30 minutes. Add the olives, season with another 2 teaspoons of salt, and continue to cook, stirring occasionally, until the liquid has reduced by a third, the meat falls off the bone, and the flavors of the stew have concentrated, about 1 hour.

Traditionally, *Carne Guisada* is served with a side of rice and beans, but it is definitely the perfect stew to spoon over a serving of noodles or *viandas majadas* (root vegetables), whole or mashed (see recipe on page 61).

Chapter IV

Soups and stews

Patitas de Cerdo con Garbanzos

Chickpea and Pig's Feet Stew

Serves 8

Ingredients:

- 5 pounds unsalted pig's feet
- 3 cups Goya Spanish tomato sauce
- 1 cup *sofrito* (see recipe on page 13)
- 1 cup Goya green olives stuffed with *pimientos*
- 4 cloves garlic, sliced into thin slivers
- 10 ounces *chorizo*, sliced into ¼-inch pieces
- 3 16-ounce cans Goya *garbanzo* beans (chickpeas), drained
- 2 ears of corn, sliced into ½-inch pieces
- 4 Idaho potatoes, peeled and cut into 1-inch cubes
- 1¼ pounds *calabaza* (Caribbean Pumpkin), peeled, seeds removed, and cut into 1-inch cubes
- 5 tablespoons salt

Procedure:

1 Boil the pig's feet: Place the pig's feet in a large stock pot, and add enough cold water to cover the pig's feet by 3 inches. Bring to a boil, cover, and cook for about 1½ hours until the meat is tender to the bite and the liquid has reduced significantly.

2 Prepare the stew: Add 3 quarts of water to the stock pot along with the tomato sauce, *sofrito*, olives, garlic slivers, *chorizo, garbanzo* beans, corn, potatoes and *calabaza*. Stir well, and bring to a boil. Cook for about 30 minutes, stirring occasionally so that the starches from the root vegetables, *garbanzos* and corn do not settle to the bottom and scorch the pot. Because the *patitas* and the *chorizo* are high in fat, make sure to skim off the impurities and fat that rise to the surface of the stew during boiling, to end up with a lighter product.

3 Reduce the heat, season the stew with 5 tablespoons of salt, and continue to simmer for another 30 minutes until the flavors have concentrated, and the liquid has thickened. Remove the pot from the heat, and set aside to rest for about 20 minutes. Stir before serving. Serve by itself as a stew, or with a side of white rice.

Patitas de Cerdo are meant for a countryside laid-back kind of gathering; they sure can be messy. Nevertheless, this recipe is as authentic as they come and a true example of a smart usage of available ingredients.

Chapter IV

Soups and stews

Tasajo
Dried Salted Beef Stew
Serves 6

Ingredients:

- 4 pounds dried *tasajo* (dried salted beef)
- 3 tablespoons Goya olive oil (not extra virgin)
- 1 onion, julienne
- 2 red Bell peppers, seeds and inner white ribbings removed, julienne
- 4 cloves garlic, pounded to a paste
- ⅔ cup *sofrito* (see recipe on page 13)
- ⅓ cup white vinegar
- 3 cups Goya Spanish tomato sauce

Procedure:

1 Place the *tasajo* in a pot, and add enough water to cover it by 6 inches. Bring to a rolling simmer, and cook for about 4 hours, adding water if necessary. Drain the *tasajo*, and set aside to cool. Remove and discard the excess fat from the beef. Using your hands, and pulling string by string, shred the beef and set aside.

2 In a large sauté pan over medium-high heat, warm the olive oil. Add the onion, red pepper, garlic and *sofrito*, and cook until the onions are wilted but still have a firm bite, about 3 minutes.

3 Deglaze with the vinegar, and cook for 2 minutes until the vinegar starts to evaporate. Stir in the tomato sauce, and cook for another 3 minutes. Add the shredded beef, and pour in 1½ quarts of water. Stir, and bring to a full boil. Reduce the heat, and cook slowly for about 2 hours, stirring occasionally, until the meat has reconstituted and the stew has thickened. Serve hot with a side of rice, *mofongo* (see recipe on page 57) or *tostones* (see recipe on page 47).

Because of the high salt content of the beef product in this recipe, we strongly suggest tasting the stew before adjusting seasonings.

For a tasty breakfast or a quick lunch, scramble a couple of eggs into a serving of stewed tasajo.

andules garbanzos **jamonilla** maíz j
ollo **salchichas** habichuelas esp
rroz gandules **garbanzos** jamoni
onganiza pollo salchichas habic
ña **arroz** gandules garbanzos jamo
onganiza **pollo salchichas** hab
ueti **lasaña** arroz gandules garba
a maíz **jueyes longaniza** pollo
s espagueti **lasaña arroz** gandules
maíz **jueyes** longaniza **pollo** salo
spagueti **lasaña** arroz gandules
a maíz **jueyes longaniza** pollo
s espagueti **lasaña arroz** gandules

Chapter V

Rice, grains and pasta

Rice, Grains & Pastas

If one thing is certain about the everyday Puerto Rico diet, it is that we know we will be having some sort of rice during the day, whether plain white rice, rice and beans (which itself can have many variations), more complex recipes, or even full rice meals, such as *Arroz con Pollo*.

At first glance it may seem incredibly simple to cook a pot of white rice, but it can be tricky if you want your rice to come out grainy and perfectly cooked. We are very particular with our rice and there is no appreciation for under-cooked or over-cooked rice. We will accept only perfectly cooked rice.

I have been cooking professionally for since 1982 and this is the chapter that took the most testing in order to provide you with sure-fire recipes. If you stir it too much, rice becomes mushy and sticky; if under-stirred, some grains may remain undercooked, and so on.

Once you perfect the classic white rice, you can always experiment, since rice is such a versatile product and is present in almost every culture.

In Puerto Rico, we favor short grain rice, which is the absolute hardest to master. As a matter of fact, despite the triple testing provided for every recipe contained in this book, if you find yourself not achieving the level of perfection expected with my rice recipes, before giving up it would be a good idea to try them with long grain rice and work yourself up towards mastering the short grain kind.

As a young chef I was awestruck as I watched the kitchen staff in the Governor's Mansion kitchen cook twenty-five pounds of rice without measuring the liquid and simply pouring water in and using a standing spoon to gauge the amount required. Once you master it, it never fails, but it took me years to get barely close to this talent, so measuring is still highly recommended.

Some schools of thought insist on washing the rice and depleting some of the excess starch. Others don't. Some insist on exclusively cooking the rice in cauldrons or *calderos*. Others are not as particular. Either way, a great pot of rice always gets compliments and is recognized as a true art.

There is no rice complete without its accompanying grain to moisten the whole deal. Sometimes the grains are substantial, as in the case of chickpeas, which are traditionally stewed with *chorizo*. Frankly, they are first courses on their own. If I had to mention the one grain that better represents us, it is the *gandul*, which is consumed throughout the year, but the Christmas season provides the best stage for everything related to pigeon peas. Very earthlike in taste,

(continued)

they greatly compare to lentils in texture and flavor.

Another classic combination in the grain department is white beans, ham, and Caribbean Pumpkin pieces with their skins still on. Since the time it takes to soften the beans also softens the pumpkin skins and thickens the bean broth simultaneously, you can eat the whole dish. It provides an excellent combination of flavors that ranges from smoked from the ham, sweet from the pumpkins and starchy from the beans.

As in many other countries, we have our share of recipes that, although not originally from our culture, are staples of our everyday kitchen. Lasagna is one of those and one that has undergone its own process of reinvention. For instance, some recipes, like my mother's delicious version, include cream cheese, which I simply adore. Others use Creole sauce instead of marinara sauce. One thing is certain, all versions of that great classic are rich and flavorful, to say the least.

In our culture, double starch and protein are the preferred combination instead of a more balanced approach. Where else in the planet would a piece of meat lasagna be served with a side of white rice and fried ripe plantains or *tostones*. The plantain part is more rational to me, but try the rice as previously suggested and who knows, maybe there will be some converts.

Our personal preference for pasta is that it not necessarily be eaten *al dente*, as suggested by the Italians, although certainly appreciated that way by many.

Our *criollo* versions are a marriage of rustic stews and pasta. Although to the eye they may look exactly like their Italian counterparts, your taste buds will reveal a taste of Puerto Rico in every bite.

> **Chapter V**
>
> Rice, grains and pasta

Arroz Blanco

White Rice
Serves 6

Despite this being a simple 4-ingredient recipe, you will find that cooking rice is an art form, more so than any other recipe found in this book. Achieving a loose grain, without undercooking or overcooking the rice, can become a labor of love.

There are numerous conventional and unconventional methods to achieving perfectly cooked rice, from balancing a spoon in the center of the *caldero* to measuring the exact ratio of rice to liquid, to giving the rice one quick stir before covering the *caldero*.

Myths and spoons aside, rice is the complement of choice in our gastronomic culture. Dressed with beans, stewed with meats and legumes, or on its own, it is consumed on a regular basis… and then some.

Ingredients:
- 2 tablespoons vegetable oil
- 3 cups medium-grain rice
- 2 tablespoons kosher salt
- 4½ cups water

Procedure:

1. In a *caldero* or a heavy-bottomed pot over high heat, warm the vegetable oil. Add the rice, and stir until the grains are well coated with the oil. Shake the *caldero* so that the rice settles evenly to the bottom of the pan.

2. Pour in 4½ cups of water, season with the salt, and stir. Bring to a full boil, and cook until the water evaporates and the surface of the rice is visible with some bubbling in between the grains, about 6 minutes.

3. Lower the heat, cover with a tight-fitting lid, and cook undisturbed until all the liquid has evaporated and the grains of rice are loose and fully cooked, 15 to 20 minutes. Remove the lid, and stir the rice with a fork before serving.

Chapter V

Rice, grains and pasta

Arroz con Gandules

Rice with Pigeon Peas
Serves 6 to 8

Ingredients:

- 3 tablespoons *achiote* oil (see recipe on page 6)
- 6 ounces cooking ham, diced
- 1 small onion, diced
- 1 cubanelle pepper, seeds and inner white ribbings removed, diced
- 4 cloves garlic, pounded to a paste
- 3 tablespoons *sofrito* (see recipe on page 13)
- 3 tablespoons Goya Spanish tomato sauce
- 3 tablespoons chopped *culantro*
- ¼ cup Goya green olives stuffed with *pimientos*
- 1 tablespoon capers
- 2 15-oz. cans of Goya *gandules* (pigeon peas), drained
- 4 cups medium-grain rice
- 5 cups chicken stock (see recipe on page 72)
- 2 tablespoons kosher salt
- 2 tablespoons Goya olive oil (not extra virgin)
- 2 large plantain leaves

Procedure:

1 In a *caldero* or a heavy-bottomed pot over high heat, warm the *achiote* oil. Add the ham, onion, pepper, garlic and *sofrito*, and cook for about 3 minutes until the onion is translucent and loses its raw taste. Stir in the tomato sauce, *culantro*, olives and capers, and cook for another 2 minutes. Stir in the drained pigeon peas.

2 Add the rice and pour in the chicken stock. Season with salt, drizzle with olive oil, and stir. Bring to a full boil, and cook until water evaporates and the surface of the rice is visible with some bubbling in between the grains, about 10 minutes.

3 Lower the heat, and place the plantain leaves over the rice (the leaves provide a wonderful addition of flavor while they aid in containing the steam needed for cooking the rice). Cover with a tight-fitting lid, and lower the heat. Cook for about 20 minutes until the all the liquid has been absorbed and the rice grains are loose and fully cooked.

Rice with Chickpeas and *Chorizo*

Serves 6 to 8

Arroz con Garbanzos y Chorizo

Ingredients:

- 2 tablespoons *achiote* oil (see recipe on page 6)
- 6 ounces *chorizo*, quartered lengthwise and sliced into ¼-inch-thick pieces
- 8 cloves garlic, pounded to a paste
- ½ cup *sofrito* (see recipe on page 13)
- 2 16-ounce cans Goya *garbanzo* beans, drained
- 3 cups medium-grain rice
- 2 tablespoons kosher salt
- 4 tablespoons Goya extra virgin olive oil

Procedure:

1 In a *caldero* or a heavy-bottomed pot over high heat, warm the *achiote* oil. Add the *chorizo* and cook for about 2 minutes to render some fat.

2 Add the garlic and *sofrito*, and cook, stirring, for another minute without browning. Stir in the *garbanzo* beans and the rice, and pour in 4½ cups of water. Season with the salt, and stir well. Bring to a full boil, and cook until the water evaporates and the surface of the rice is visible with some bubbling in between the grains, about 6 minutes

3 Cover with a tight-fitting lid, and lower the heat. Cook for about 20 minutes until all the liquid has been absorbed and the rice grains are loose and fully cooked. Remove the lid, drizzle the rice with the olive oil, and stir with a fork before serving.

Chapter V

Rice, grains and pasta

Arroz con Jamonilla

Rice with Luncheon Meat

Serves 6 to 8

Ingredients:

- 3 tablespoons Goya olive oil (not extra virgin)
- ½ onion, diced
- ½ cubanelle pepper, seeds and inner white ribbings removed, diced
- 1 clove garlic, pounded to a paste
- ¼ cup *sofrito* (see recipe on page 13)
- 2 tablespoons chopped *culantro*
- ¾ cup Goya Spanish tomato sauce
- ⅓ cup Goya green olives stuffed with *pimientos*
- 2 tablespoons Goya capers
- 12 ounces luncheon meat, cut into a large dice
- 3 cups medium-grain rice
- 4½ cups chicken stock (see recipe on page 72)
- 1 tablespoon kosher salt
- Goya extra virgin olive oil for drizzling

Procedure:

1 In a *caldero* or a heavy-bottomed pot over high heat, warm the olive oil. Add the onion, pepper, garlic, *sofrito* and *culantro*, and cook, stirring, until the onion has softened and has lost its raw taste, about 3 minutes. Add the tomato sauce, olives and capers, and cook for another 2 minutes, stirring so the ingredients do not stick to the bottom of the pan. Add the luncheon meat and cook for 2 minutes, stirring carefully to avoid mashing the meat.

2 Add the rice, and stir to coat with the sauce. Pour in the chicken stock, season with the salt and stir. Bring to a full boil, and cook for about 10 minutes, until the water evaporates and the surface of the rice is visible, bubbling in between the grains.

3 Lower the heat, drizzle with extra virgin olive oil, and cover with a tight-fitting lid. Cook for 25 minutes until all the liquid has been absorbed and the rice grains are loose and fully cooked.

Arroz con Maíz

Rice with Corn

Serves 6 to 8

Ingredients:

- 4 ounces unsalted butter
- 1 small onion, diced
- ½ red Bell pepper, seeds and inner white ribbings removed, diced
- 3 cups sweet corn kernels
- 3 tablespoons chopped *culantro*
- 3 cups medium-grain rice
- 2 tablespoons kosher salt
- 1 tablespoon sugar
- 4½ cups water

Procedure:

1 In a *caldero* or heavy-bottomed pot over medium-high heat, melt the butter. When it starts foaming, add the onion, red pepper, the corn kernels and *culantro*. Cook for about 3 minutes until the onion is translucent and loses its raw flavor.

2 Add the rice, and stir so it is coated with the other ingredients. Pour in 4½ cups of water, season with the salt and sugar, and stir. Bring to a full boil, and cook until the water evaporates and the surface of the rice is visible with some bubbling in between the grains, about 6 minutes.

3 Lower the heat, and cover with a tight-fitting lid. Cook for 20 to 25 minutes until all the liquid has been absorbed and rice grains are loose and fully cooked. Remove the lid, and stir with a fork before serving.

> **Chapter V**
>
> Rice, grains and pasta

Arroz con Jueyes

Rice with Crab Meat
Serves 6 to 8

Ingredients:

- 3 tablespoons Goya olive oil (not extra virgin)
- 2 tablespoons *achiote* oil
- 3 ounces *tocino*, cut into fine dice
- ½ onion, cut into fine dice
- ½ cubanelle pepper, seeds and inner white ribbings removed, cut into fine dice
- 8 cloves garlic, pounded to a paste
- ¼ cup *sofrito* (see recipe on page 13)
- 1 cup Goya Spanish tomato sauce
- 2 tablespoons Goya capers
- 1 pound blue crab claw meat
- 4 tablespoons kosher salt
- 5 cups medium-grain rice
- 3 cups chicken stock (see recipe on page 72)
- 3 tablespoons chopped *culantro*
- 3 cups water

Procedure:

1 In a *caldero* or a heavy-bottomed pot over high heat, warm the olive oil with the *achiote* oil. Add the *tocino*, and cook for about 3 minutes until it starts rendering its fat and melting away. Add the onion, pepper, garlic and *sofrito*, and cook, stirring until the onion is soft and loses its raw taste, about 3 minutes. Add the tomato sauce and capers, and cook for another 2 minutes, stirring so the sauce does not stick to the bottom of the pan. Stir in the crab meat, season with ½ teaspoon of salt, and cook for another 2 minutes.

2 Stir in the rice, and pour in the chicken stock and 3 cups of water. Season with 3 tablespoons of salt, and bring to a full boil. Cook until the water evaporates and the surface of the rice is visible with some bubbling in-between the grains, about 7 minutes.

3 Lower the heat, cover with a tight-fitting lid, and cook undisturbed until all the liquid has evaporated and the grains of rice are loose and fully cooked, about 20 minutes. Remove the lid, add the *culantro*, and stir the rice with a fork before serving.

Chapter V

Rice, grains and pasta

Arroz con Longaniza

Rice with "Longaniza" Sausage

Serves 6 to 8

Ingredients:

- 1 pound *longaniza* sausage, casings removed
- 1 onion, diced
- 4 cloves garlic, pounded to a paste
- ¼ cup *sofrito* (see recipe on page 13)
- 5 tablespoons chopped *culantro*
- 3 cups medium-grain rice
- 2 tablespoons kosher salt
- 4½ cups water

Procedure:

1. Place the *longaniza* in a *caldero* or a heavy-bottomed pot over high heat and cook for about 4 minutes until it renders fat and starts to brown, stirring and breaking the *longaniza* apart with a wooden spoon as it cooks.

2. Add the onion, garlic, *sofrito* and 2 tablespoons of *culantro* and cook, stirring, for another 4 minutes until the onion is translucent and loses its raw taste. Add the rice, and stir to coat with the rest of the ingredients. Pour in 4½ cups of water, season with the salt, and stir, scraping any browned bits from the bottom of the *caldero*. Bring to a full boil and cook until the water evaporates and the surface of the rice is visible with some bubbling in between the grains, about 6 minutes.

3. Lower the heat, and cover with a tight-fitting lid. Cook until all the liquid has been absorbed and the rice grains are loose and fully cooked, 25 to 30 minutes. Using a fork, stir in the remaining 2 tablespoons of *culantro*.

Arroz con Pollo

Chapter V

Rice, grains and pasta

Rice with Chicken

Serves 6 to 8

Ingredients:

- 3 tablespoons *achiote* oil (see recipe on page 6)
- ½ onion, diced
- ½ red Bell pepper, seeds and inner white ribbings removed, diced
- 4 cloves garlic, pounded to a paste
- ½ cup *sofrito* (see recipe on page 13)
- 3 tablespoons Goya Spanish tomato sauce
- 4 tablespoons chopped *culantro*, divided
- ½ cup Goya green olives stuffed with *pimientos*
- 2 tablespoon Goya capers
- 1½ lbs. skinless, boneless chicken thighs, cut into strips
- 1 cup dry cooking sherry
- 4 cups medium-grain rice
- 5 cups chicken stock (see recipe on page 72)
- 3 tablespoons kosher salt
- 1 cup shelled green peas
- 4 tablespoons Goya olive oil (not extra virgin)

In my early years of *Arroz con Pollo* consumption, I tended to be quite picky about the integrity of the dish. It is probable that if there wasn't someone volunteering to remove the skin and the bones from the chicken in the *arroz*, I would not eat it. Perhaps this is why I choose to prepare *Arroz con Pollo* in a way that won't alter its authenticity yet will save me and others the task of removing the skin and bones as opposed to missing out on the whole experience.

Traditionally, a whole chicken is hacked away at and cooked into the rice (skin and bones and all), providing all the elements needed to flavor the liquid of the rice as it cooks. I opted to use boneless and skinless chicken, yet I added chicken stock to make up for those missing elements.

Procedure:

1 In a *caldero* or a heavy-bottomed pot over high heat, warm the *achiote* oil. Add the onion, red pepper, garlic and *sofrito*, and cook until the onion is translucent and loses its raw taste, about 3 minutes. Add the tomato sauce, 2 tablespoons of *culantro*, the olives and capers, and cook for another 3 minutes, stirring so that the sauce doesn't stick to the bottom.

2 Add the chicken, and cook for 2 minutes. Deglaze with the wine, and cook until it evaporates, about 4 minutes. Add the rice, and stir well to coat with the rest of the ingredients. Pour in the chicken stock, season with the salt, and stir. Bring to a full boil and cook until the water evaporates and the surface of the rice is visible with some bubbling in between the grains, about 8 minutes.

3 Lower the heat, and cover with a tight-fitting lid. Cook until all the liquid has been absorbed and the rice grains are loose and fully cooked, about 20 minutes. Add the peas, cover and cook for another 3 minutes. Drizzle with 4 tablespoons of olive oil and, using a fork, stir, in the remaining 2 tablespoons of *culantro*. Serve with a side of *habichuelas rojas* (see recipe on page 133).

Chapter V

Rice, grains and pasta

Arroz con Salchichas

Rice with Vienna Sausages

Serves 6 to 8

Ingredients:

- 2 tablespoons *achiote* oil (see recipe on page *6*)
- ½ onion, diced
- 4 cloves garlic, pounded to a paste
- 6 tablespoons chopped *culantro*, divided
- ½ cup *sofrito* (see recipe on page *13*)
- 3 tablespoons Goya Spanish tomato sauce
- ¼ cup Goya green olives stuffed with *pimientos*
- 1 tablespoon Goya capers
- 3 5-ounce cans Vienna sausage, sliced into ½-inch pieces
- 3 cups medium-grain rice
- 2 tablespoons salt
- 4½ cups water

Despite the years I've spent educating my palate to the finer things and as much as I adore and respect *haute cuisine*, like many Puerto Ricans, I have a weakness for Vienna sausages, one that might be rooted in my adoration for my Grandmother Milagros, who made the very best *Arroz con Salchichas*.

Procedure:

1 In a *caldero* over high heat, warm the *achiote* oil. Add the onion, garlic, 4 tablespoons of *culantro*, and *sofrito* and cook for about 3 minutes, until the onion is translucent and loses its raw taste. Add the tomato sauce, olives and capers, and cook for another 2 minutes, stirring so that the sauce doesn't stick to the bottom.

2 Add the Vienna sausages and the rice and stir carefully to avoid breaking the sausages. Pour in 4½ cups of water, season with the salt, and stir. Bring to a full boil and cook until the water evaporates and the surface of the rice is visible with some bubbling in between the grains, about 8 minutes.

3 Lower the heat, and cover with a tight-fitting lid. Cook until the all the liquid has been absorbed and the rice grains are loose and fully cooked, about 20 minutes. Using a fork, stir in the remaining 2 tablespoons of *culantro*. Serve with a side of *habichuelas blancas* (see recipe on page 131).

> Chapter V
>
> Rice, grains and pasta

Arroz Relleno

Many of the recipes contained in this book have nostalgic values for me. But of all the recipes, *Arroz Relleno* has got to be the one that I request the most of my mother, and one that my sisters and I, to this day, still look forward to when our mother prepares it.

Stuffed Rice
Serves 6 to 8

Ingredients:
- *Fricasé de Pollo* (see recipe on page 97)
- 4 cups cooked medium-grain rice
- 1 pound thinly sliced Swiss cheese

Procedure:

1 Preheat the oven to 300°F. Place the chicken *fricasé* in a colander, and set the strained sauce aside. Remove the chicken pieces from the colander, and set aside. Remove and discard the bones and any excess fat from the pieces of chicken. Using your hands, thinly shred the chicken, and mix with the rice.

2 Spread ⅓ of the rice-chicken mixture on the bottom of a baking dish, and using your hands or a rubber spatula, press down to form a tight even layer. Pour 1 cup of the reserved *fricasé* sauce over the layer of rice, arrange half of the cheese slices on top, and spread another ½ cup of the sauce over the cheese. Spread the remaining rice in a layer on top, and pack down to tighten. Pour the remaining sauce over the rice, and arrange the remaining cheese on top.

3 Place in the oven, and bake until the cheese melts and develops a golden hue, about 30 minutes. Remove from the oven, slice as you would a lasagna, and serve.

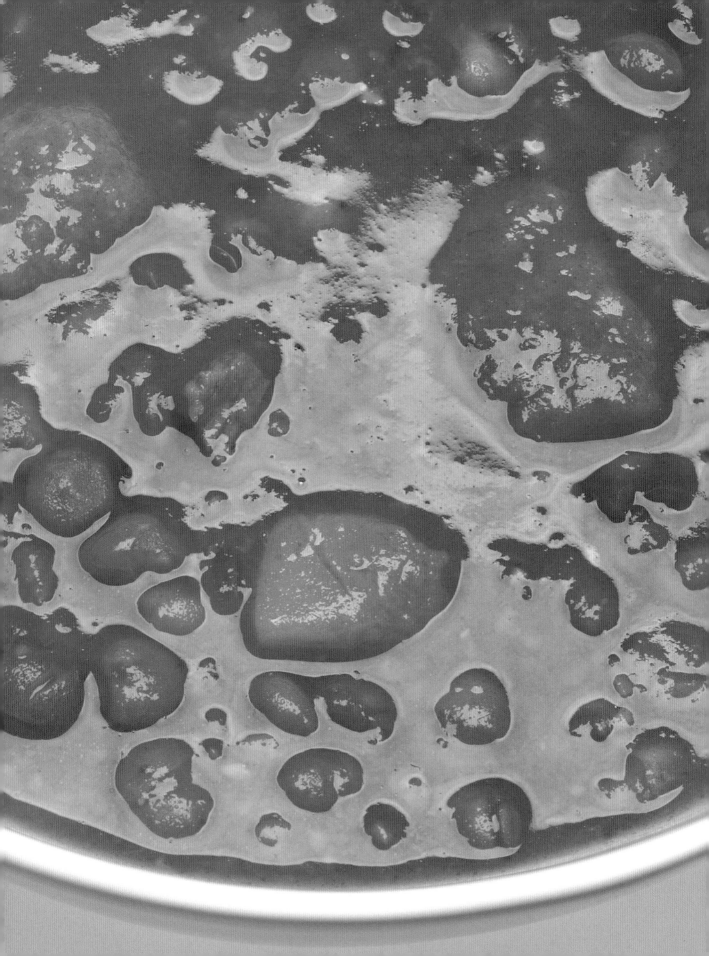

> **Chapter V**
>
> Rice, grains and pasta

Gandules
con Bolitas de Plátano

Pigeon Peas with Plantain Dumplings
Serves 6

Ingredients:

For the *bolitas*:
- 2 green plantains, peeled
- 2½ tablespoons Goya olive oil (not extra virgin)
- 1 teaspoon *adobo* (see recipe on page 6)
- 1 teaspoon kosher salt

For the *gandules*:
- 3 tablespoons Goya olive oil
- 4 ounces cooking ham, diced
- 1 onion, diced
- ½ cubanelle pepper, seeds and inner white ribbings removed, diced
- 4 garlic cloves, pounded to a paste
- ½ cup *sofrito* (see recipe on page 13)
- 1 cup Goya Spanish tomato sauce
- 4 15-ounce cans Goya pigeon peas, drained
- 6 ounces *calabaza* (Caribbean Pumpkin), peeled and seeds removed, cut into large dice
- 3 quarts chicken stock (see recipe on page 72)
- 2 Goya bay leaves
- 2 tablespoons kosher salt

Procedure:

1 Prepare the *bolitas*: Grate the plantains through the smallest holes of a grater to obtain a moist paste. Transfer to a bowl, and combine with the olive oil, *adobo* and salt. Mix well, and form into small balls, about 1 tablespoon worth of paste (2 plantains should yield about a dozen *bolitas*). Cover so they don't oxidize, and set aside.

2 Prepare the *gandules*: In a large heavy-bottomed pot over medium-high heat, warm the olive oil. Add the ham along with the onion, pepper, garlic and *sofrito* and cook, stirring, for about 3 minutes until the onion is translucent and loses its raw taste. Add the tomato sauce, and cook for another 4 minutes, stirring so that the ingredients do not stick to the bottom of the pot.

3 Stir in the *gandules* and *calabaza*, pour in the chicken stock, and add the bay leaves. Season with the salt, bring to a full boil, and cook for about 15 minutes.

4 Carefully add the *bolitas* one by one and scatter throughout the stew. After 5 minutes, stir to ensure the *bolitas* maintain their round shape. Reduce the heat, and cook for another 45 minutes until the stew has thickened, and the *bolitas* are cooked through. Remove from the heat, remove and discard the bay leaves, and serve on its own or with a side of white rice.

I recommend using canned pigeon peas because, even in Puerto Rico, the access to fresh ones is limited. These present a reasonable alternative and it allows for preparing the recipe year-round.

> **Chapter V**
>
> Rice, grains and pasta

Garbanzos
Guisados con Chorizo

Stewed Chickpeas with "*Chorizo*"
Serves 6 to 8

Ingredients:

- 5 tablespoons Goya olive oil (not extra virgin)
- 10 ounces *chorizo*, diced
- 1 onion, diced
- 4 cloves garlic, pounded to a paste
- 1 cubanelle pepper, seeds and white ribbing removed, diced
- 1 cup *sofrito* (see recipe on page 13)
- 1 cup Goya Spanish tomato sauce
- 1 pound dried Goya *garbanzo* beans, soaked in water overnight, drained
- 8 ounces *calabaza* (Caribbean Pumpkin), peeled and seeds removed, cubed
- 1 Idaho potato, peeled and cubed
- ⅓ cup Goya green olives stuffed with *pimientos*
- 4 tablespoons chopped *culantro*
- 4 quarts chicken stock (see recipe on page 72)

Procedure:

1. In a large heavy-bottomed pot over high heat, warm the olive oil. Add the *chorizo*, onion, garlic, pepper and *sofrito* and cook until the onion is translucent and loses its raw taste, about 4 minutes. Stir in the tomato sauce, and cook for another minute, stirring so the ingredients do not stick to the bottom of the pot.

2. Add the *garbanzo* beans along with the *calabaza*, potato, olives and *culantro*. Pour in the chicken stock, and stir well. Bring to a full boil, and cook for about 20 minutes, stirring occasionally. Reduce the heat, and simmer for another hour until the *garbanzos* are tender yet firm to the bite, the flavors have concentrated and the stew has thickened.

> Chapter V
>
> Rice, grains and pasta

Habichuelas
Blancas Guisadas

Stewed White Beans
Serves 6 to 8

Ingredients:

- 5 tablespoons Goya olive oil (not extra virgin)
- ½ onion, diced
- ½ cubanelle pepper, seeds and inner white ribbings removed, diced
- 4 cloves garlic, pounded to a paste
- 1 cup *sofrito* (see recipe on page 13)
- 4 ounces smoked ham, diced
- 3½ cups Goya Spanish tomato sauce
- 5 tablespoons chopped *culantro*
- 1 Idaho potato, peeled and cut into large dice
- 8 ounces *calabaza* (Caribbean Pumpking), peeled and seeded, cut into large dice
- 1 pound Goya dried small white beans, soaked in water overnight, drained
- 3 tablespoons kosher salt
- 3¼ quarts water

Procedure:

1. In a large heavy-bottomed pot over high heat, warm the olive oil. Add the onion, pepper, garlic, *sofrito* and the ham and cook for about 3 minutes until the onion is translucent and loses its raw taste and the ham renders some of its fat. Stir in the tomato sauce and the *culantro* and cook for another 2 minutes, stirring so the ingredients do not stick to the bottom of the pot.

2. Add the potato and the *calabaza*, stir, and cook for another 3 minutes. Add the beans, pour in 3½ quarts of water, season with the salt, and stir well. Bring to a full boil and cook for about 4 minutes. Lower the heat, and simmer for about 1½ hours, stirring occasionally so that the starches do not stick to the bottom and scorch. Serve hot over rice.

> Chapter V
>
> Rice, grains and pasta

Habichuelas Rojas Guisadas

Stewed Red Kidney Beans
Serves 6 to 8

Ingredients:
- 5 tablespoons Goya olive oil (not extra virgin)
- ½ onion, diced
- ½ cubanelle pepper, seeds and inner white ribbing removed, diced
- 4 cloves garlic, pounded to a paste
- ½ cup *sofrito*
- 4 ounces smoked ham, diced
- 1½ cups Goya Spanish tomato sauce
- 3 tablespoons chopped *culantro*
- 1 Idaho potato, peeled and cut into large dice
- 8 ounces *calabaza* (Caribbean Pumpkin), peeled and seeded, cut into large dice
- 1 pound Goya dried red kidney beans, soaked in water overnight, drained
- 2 tablespoons kosher salt
- 3½ quarts water

Procedure:

1 In a large heavy-bottomed pot over high heat, warm the olive oil. Add the onion, pepper, garlic, *sofrito* and the ham, and cook for about 3 minutes until the onion is translucent and loses its raw taste and the ham renders some of its fat. Stir in the tomato sauce and the *culantro*, and cook for another 2 minutes, stirring so the ingredients do not stick to the bottom of the pot.

2 Add the potato and the *calabaza*, stir, and cook for another 3 minutes. Add the beans, pour in 3½ quarts of water, season with the salt, and stir well. Bring to a full boil and cook for about 4 minutes. Lower the heat and simmer for about 1½ hours, stirring occasionally so that the starches do not stick to the bottom and scorch. Serve hot over rice.

Chapter V

Rice, grains and pasta

Espagueti con Carne Criolla

"*Criollo*" style Spaghetti with Meat Sauce

Serves 8-10

Ingredients:

- 2 tablespoons olive oil (not extra virgin)
- ½ onion, diced
- 1 clove garlic, pounded to a paste
- 2 tablespoons *sofrito* (see recipe on page 13)
- 3 tablespoons chopped *culantro*
- 1 cup dry cooking sherry
- 3 cups spaghetti sauce
- 1 teaspoon Goya dried oregano
- 1 teaspoon kosher salt
- 2 teaspoons sugar
- 1 pound thick spaghetti
- 3 cups *picadillo* (see recipe on page 167)
- 1 tablespoon chopped basil

Procedure:

1 Prepare the marinara sauce: In a saucepan over medium-high heat, warm the olive oil. Add the onion, garlic, *sofrito* and *culantro* and cook until the onion is translucent and loses its raw taste, about 4 minutes. Deglaze with the wine, and cook until it starts to evaporate, about 4 minutes. Add the spaghetti sauce and the oregano, and season with the salt and sugar. Cook for about 15 minutes, stirring occasionally, until the flavors concentrate and the sauce starts to reduce.

2 Meanwhile, cook the *pasta*: Bring a large pot of water to a boil and add salt generously. It should taste as salty as sea water. Add the *pasta*, and cook for about 10 minutes until the pasta is soft (*al dente* is not really a priority when making criollo-style pasta dishes).

3 Add the *picadillo* and the basil to the marinara sauce, and stir well. Drain the pasta, and add to the meat sauce. Toss well (it is important that the *pasta* be well coated with the sauce and bits of meat), and serve.

Because *al dente* is not a concern in *criollo* pastas, leftovers of this dish make a great middle-of-the-night snack, reheated or straight out-of-the-fridge cold.

Chapter V

Rice, grains and pasta

"*Criollo*" style Spaghetti with Chicken
Serves 8-10

Espagueti con Pollo Criollo

Ingredients:

- one full recipe *Fricasé de Pollo* (see recipe on page 97)
- 2 tablespoons Goya olive oil (not extra virgin)
- ½ onion, diced
- 1 clove garlic, pounded to a paste
- 2 tablespoons *sofrito* (see recipe on page 13)
- 3 tablespoons chopped *culantro*
- 1 cup dry cooking sherry
- 1½ cups spaghetti sauce
- 1 teaspoon Goya dried oregano
- 1 teaspoon kosher salt
- 1 teaspoon sugar
- 1 pound thick spaghetti
- 1 tablespoon chopped basil

Procedure:

1. Place the chicken *fricasé* in a colander and set the strained sauce aside. Remove the chicken pieces from the colander and set aside. Remove and discard the bones and any excess fat from the pieces of chicken. Using your hands, thinly shred the chicken and set aside.

2. Prepare the marinara sauce: In a saucepan over medium-high heat, warm the olive oil. Add the onion, garlic, *sofrito* and *culantro*, and cook until the onion is translucent and loses its raw taste, about 4 minutes. Deglaze with the wine, and cook until it starts to evaporate, about 4 minutes. Add the spaghetti sauce and the reserved sauce from the *fricasé*. Add the oregano, and season with the salt and sugar. Cook for about 15 minutes, stirring occasionally, until the flavors concentrate and the sauce starts to reduce.

3. Meanwhile, cook the pasta: Bring a large pot of water to a boil. Add salt and the pasta and cook for about 10 minutes, until the *pasta* is soft (*al dente* is not really a priority when making *criollo*-style *pasta* dishes).

4. Add the shredded chicken and the basil to the marinara sauce and stir well. Drain the *pasta* and add to the chicken sauce. Toss well (it is important that the *pasta* be well coated with the sauce and bits of chicken), and serve.

Because al dente is not a concern in *criollo pastas*, leftovers of this dish make a great middle-of-the-night snack, reheated or straight out-of-the-fridge cold.

Chapter V

Rice, grains and pasta

Puerto Rican-Style Lasagna

Serves 6 to 8

Lasaña Criolla

Ingredients:

- 2 tablespoons Goya olive oil (not extra virgin), plus extra
- ½ onion, diced
- 1 clove garlic, pounded to a paste
- 2 tablespoons *sofrito* (see recipe on page 13)
- 4 tablespoons chopped *culantro*
- 1 cup dry cooking sherry
- 4 cups spaghetti sauce
- 1 teaspoon Goya dried oregano
- 1 tablespoon chopped basil
- 1 teaspoon kosher salt
- 2 teaspoons sugar
- 1 pound uncooked lasagna noodles
- 6 cups *picadillo* (see recipe on page 167)
- 8 ounces cream cheese, in pieces
- 2 peeled ripe plantains, diced and fried
- 1½ pounds thinly sliced Provolone cheese

Pasta dishes are common in local diners. They are a hearty alternative to using leftovers from chicken stew and *picadillo*. To the surprise of many outsiders, these starchy dishes tend to defy the rules of common sense in our culture: they are served with a side of white rice!

Procedure:

1 Prepare the marinara sauce: In a saucepan over medium-high heat, warm the olive oil. Add the onion, garlic, *sofrito* and *culantro*, and cook until the onion is translucent and loses its raw taste, about 4 minutes. Deglaze with the wine, and cook until it starts to evaporate, about 4 minutes. Add the spaghetti sauce, stir in the oregano and basil, and season with the salt and sugar. Cook for about 15 minutes, stirring occasionally, until the flavors concentrate and the sauce starts to reduce. Remove from the heat, and set aside to cool.

2 Meanwhile, boil the lasagna noodles: In a large wide pot, bring abundant water to a boil. Add salt and the lasagna noodles, and cook for about 12 minutes, until the noodles are soft. Drain the noodles, and transfer to a bath of ice water. Drain, and set aside.

3 Assemble the lasagna: Preheat oven to 350ºF. Brush a 12"x10" baking dish with olive oil, and arrange a layer of lasagna noodles in the bottom of the dish. Pour in 1 cup of marinara sauce, and spread to form an even layer. Layer half of the *picadillo* on top of the sauce, and dress with another ½ cup of sauce.

4 Arrange 4 ounces of the cream cheese and half of the fried plantains scattered over the meat, and cover with a layer of half the slices of Provolone. Pour in another cup of sauce over the layer of Provolone and spread out. Add a layer of the remaining *picadillo*, and pour in another cup of sauce over it (reserve remaining ½ cup of sauce for the final layer).

5 Scatter the remaining cream cheese and fried plantains on top, and cover with a layer of Provolone (reserve about 4 slices). Press down lightly to tightly pack the lasagna. Arrange a final layer of noodles and pour some sauce on top. Cut the remaining 4 slices of Provolone into pieces, and scatter over the sauced noodles.

6 Wipe the edges of the baking dish so no scorching occurs, and loosely cover with aluminum foil. Place in the oven for about 30 minutes. Remove the foil, and continue to bake for another 15 minutes until the surface of the lasagna is a deep golden color and the edges are crisp. Remove from the oven, and set aside to rest for about 10 minutes. Slice and serve.

za pollo al horno pollo frito pa
panada **churrasco carne** fr
jamón carne mechada longa
llo frito **pavo** chuletas bistec
rne **frita** picadillo **chayote**
onganiza pollo al horno poll
stec empanada **churrasco** c
yote **jamón** carne mechada
ollo frito **pavo** chuletas bistec
rne **frita** picadillo **chayote**
onganiza pollo al horno poll
stec empanada **churrasco** c

Chapter VI

Meat

Meat

Despite the amount of water surrounding Puerto Rico, meat is the preferred protein, whether in the form of a delicious suckling pig, eye round roast, BBQ chicken, beef stew, chicken *fricassée*, baked ham or *bistec encebollado*. It is almost assumed that if there is an absence of meat in a certain meal, it would not entirely qualify as a complete meal.

Pork is a favorite for its flavor and crispy skin. However, all statistics reveal beef as the preferred meat. Specifically, beef tenderloin is highly regarded but is not always on the everyday table because of its price. Then there are the cuts of meat that we have inherited through other cultures that settled in Puerto Rico.

The Argentinean community introduced us to the skirt steak or *churrasco* which, even without pulling out statistical charts, is our preferred BBQ cut of meat (due, I think, to its terrific marbling, price, and tenderness). Also, the fact that it is never a very thick cut of meat provides for our culture's general appreciation of meats when they are cooked a little over medium-well. There are, however, many of us who have evolved from the suggested (imposed?) well-done preference that our mothers and grandmothers provided.

One of the beauties of Puerto Rico is the ability to get just about every product under the sun, and meats are no exception. These days you can get Argentinean, American, Canadian, Japanese and local beef, poultry, pork and veal, among others.

In general terms, our local beef does not contain great marbling so while it is great for certain recipes, it is not so for others.

Fresh meat beats frozen any day. In that sense, depending on your temperature preference, local beef may be the right choice if you like your meats cooked medium to medium-rare, in which case the absence of marbling may be overlooked.

We love to marinate *(adobar)* our meats overnight, breaking every rule I was taught in Culinary School in regards to salting, since that method draws moisture out. But you can tell when one has a "hand" for seasoning *(adobar)* which, when successful, is always praised and considered somewhat of an art.

Crispy is always in vogue with Puerto Ricans, and to me nothing is lovelier than crispy fried pork chops or *Carne Frita*, which is nothing more than pork butt cut into chunks and marinated *(adobado)* overnight and fried until somewhat dry but very crispy. In our culture that translates into delicious crispy morsels of meat which we accentuate with pickled onions or *escabeche*. (Great with cocktails after a round of golf!)

Still, regarding crispy foods, I think that one of my fondest childhood memories is having my Grandmother Milagros' Fried Chicken. Different than many other recipes the globe has to offer, our way with chicken is without dredging in flour, so the crispiness is simply provided by a blistered chicken skin.

On the subject of chicken, nothing is as flavorful as spit-roasted chickens on the side of the road. It's said (in a joking manner) that they

(continued)

are roasted so close to the cars passing by, carbon monoxide has provided part of the flavoring.

There are sectors of our Island that have specialized in different components of our diet and when it comes to meat, it is Guavate, only forty-five minutes outside of San Juan into the central part of the Island. Guavate is the area for those of us who live in the Northeastern shore to indulge in everything pork, meaning roast pork, blood sausages, tripe, *Mondongo* (Tripe Stew) and *Cuajo*, which is pork intestines cooked until very tender and served stew-like, with white rice.

No matter your preference, what I know about meats in our *criollo* way of cooking is that they are full of flavors and tenderness when done the right way.

Chapter VI

Meat

Sándwiches de Mezcla

Luncheon Meat-mix Sandwiches

Makes about 3 dozen tea sandwiches

Ingredients:

- 16 ounces American yellow cheese
- 12 ounces luncheon meat
- one 7-ounce can roasted red peppers, juice reserved
- ¼ cup ketchup
- 4 loaves white sandwich bread

Procedure:

1 Place the cheese and luncheon meat in a food processor and process to a coarse grind. Add the roasted peppers and process until smooth. Scrape the sides of the food processor with a rubber spatula, add the ketchup and ¼ cup of the reserved juice from the roasted peppers, and process until a smooth salmon colored mixture forms.

2 Spread the mixture over half of the bread slices, top with the remaining slices, and set aside. On a clean surface, stack 2 to 3 sandwiches together. Using a serrated knife, cut and discard (or snack on) the crusts from all 4 sides of the sandwiches. Cut the sandwiches into quarters, and set aside. Repeat with the remaining sandwiches. If you are doing the sandwiches ahead of time, arrange them on trays, and cover with damp kitchen towels to prevent them from drying out.

Sándwiches de Mezcla are a staple in any Puerto Rican birthday celebration. Often, colored bread is purchased to give the sandwich a more festive look. I should also mention that these sandwiches are currently found in the lunch boxes of elementary school kids.

This is a great example of how elements of a culture, and how one was raised, still impact upon you, regardless of the evolution of your palette. There is a small shop in the building where my office is located, that has baskets of these little sandwiches prepared every day. Despite the availability of far better foods for me to consume, I still indulge from time to time.

Chapter VI

Meat

Longaniza

Criollo Pork Sausage
Yields approximately 15 pieces

If you wish to engage in the process of making *longaniza* from scratch, and have the ingredients and equipment to do so, find a charcuterie book to guide you through it. Although I applaud the effort, I suggest choosing from the commercial brands of *longaniza* available in the market, each one having its distinctive features. Some might hold their filling looser and some feel tighter. If you come across a looser piece of *longaniza*, slice it into larger pieces, so that the filling is successfully contained in its casing during baking.

Like *morcilla, longaniza* can also be prepared free of its casing. Traditional recipes such as *Pastelón de Papa* and *Piñón* can be adapted for loose *longaniza* filling. *Arroz con Longaniza* (see recipe on page 119) calls for extracting the sausage from its casing.

Ingredients:
- 1 pound *longaniza* sausage

Procedure:

1. Preheat the oven to 275°F. Slice the *longaniza* into ½-inch-thick pieces. Arrange on a sheet pan lined with parchment paper, and place in the oven. Bake for about 25 minutes until the *longaniza* tightens and is springy to the touch.

2. Remove the *longaniza* from the oven, and serve as an appetizer or snack.

This is the look of Puerto Rican style roasted chicken skin.

Chapter VI

Meat

Pollo al Horno

Roasted Chicken
Serves 4 to 6

In Puerto Rico, it is quite common to see food stands serving spit-roasted chicken alongside main roads and highways. Although it might seem unpleasant to savor food that is cooked so close to tar and speeding cars, the seasonings used and the cook's crafty hands account for some of the most flavorful spit-roasted birds I've ever tasted. This is my version of baked chicken, roadside stand-style, without the tar!

Ingredients:

- 4 tablespoons *adobo* (see recipe on page 6)
- 2 tablespoons chopped oregano
- 6 tablespoons Goya olive oil (not extra virgin)
- one whole chicken, about 5 pounds, innards removed

Procedure:

1 In a bowl, combine the *adobo* with the oregano and the olive oil, and mix well. Carefully separate the skin from the flesh of the chicken without tearing it. Rub the *adobo* mixture inside the skin and all over the outside of the whole chicken. Set aside in the refrigerator to marinate for 1 hour to overnight.

2 Preheat oven to 350ºF. Truss the chicken by tucking the wings behind the breast. Place on a baking rack over a baking sheet. Place in heated oven for about 1 hour and 15 minutes, until the chicken's juices run clean and the skin is crisp and a deep golden color. If the color of the chicken skin is too light, for additional color you can place the chicken back in the oven at 400ºF, watching it closely, for 5-7 minutes. Remove from the oven, and set aside to rest for at least 10 minutes before carving.

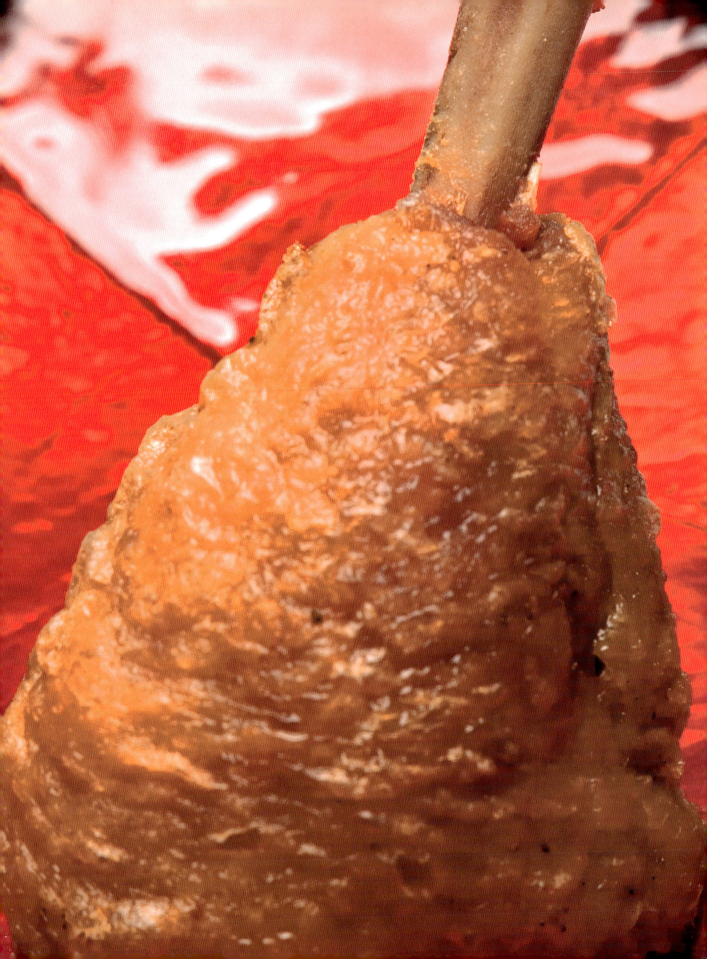

Chapter VI

Meat

Pollo Frito

Fried chicken
Serves 4 to 6

Ingredients:
- one whole chicken, about 4½ pounds, innards removed
- 3 tablespoons *adobo* (see recipe on page 6)
- 2 tablespoons chopped oregano
- 6 tablespoons Goya olive oil (not extra virgin)
- vegetable oil for frying

Procedure:

1. Separate the chicken into parts: With a sharp knife, remove the wings, thighs and drumsticks from the chicken and set aside. Separate the drumsticks from the thighs and set aside. Cut out the chicken's backbone entirely (discard or reserve for chicken stock if desired). Cut each breast in half crosswise, being careful not to tear the skin. Transfer with the other chicken parts into a bowl and set aside.

2. In a separate bowl, combine the *adobo,* oregano and olive oil and mix well. Pour this mixture over the chicken parts and toss to completely coat all the pieces. Cover and set aside in the refrigerator to marinate for at least 1 hour. If time allows, marinate overnight.

3. In a deep fryer or in a skillet, heat about 3 inches of vegetable oil to 350°F. Add the chicken parts to the hot oil, and fry for about 15-20 minutes until the skin is crispy -blistering- and a deep golden color. Remove from the oil, and set aside to drain on paper towels. Serve hot.

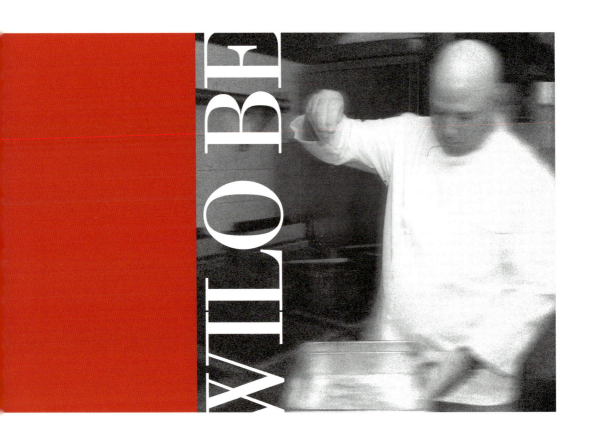

> **Chapter VI**
>
> Meat

Pavo Criollo al Horno

Puerto Rican-style Roast Turkey

Serves 8 to 10

Ingredients:

- 8 cloves garlic
- 1 small onion, chopped
- ½ cup chopped oregano
- 3 tablespoons *adobo* (see recipe on page 6)
- 2 cups Goya olive oil (not extra virgin)
- 1 whole turkey, about 14 pounds, innards removed
- 1 pound butter, cut into small pieces

Procedure:

1 Prepare the marinade: In a food processor, combine the garlic, onion and oregano and process down to a paste. Transfer to a bowl and combine with the *adobo* and the olive oil. Mix well, and set aside.

2 Carefully separate the skin from the flesh of the turkey without tearing it. Rub some of the marinade inside the turkey's skin, and insert the pieces of butter in between the skin and the flesh. Rub the remaining marinade all over the turkey's skin.

3 Truss the bird, and set aside in the refrigerator to marinate overnight. Remove the turkey from the refrigerator, and set aside to come to room temperature.

4 Preheat the oven to 325°F. Transfer the turkey to a roasting rack, and place over a baking pan. Place in the oven, and roast for 3 to 3¼ hours until the turkey's juices run clear and the skin starts to crisp and is a light golden color. Remove from the oven and set aside to rest for about 20 minutes before carving.

Chapter VI

Meat

Chuletas Fritas

Fried Pork Chops
Serves 4

Although I have an appreciation for juicy pork, even slightly underdone tenderloin, I still can't get enough of thin, crispy, salty and dried out fried pork chops. The mere mention of these makes my mouth water, just as *foie gras* would!

Ingredients:

- 1 tablespoon *adobo* (see recipe on page 6)
- ¼ teaspoon freshly ground black pepper
- 2 cloves garlic, pounded to a paste
- 1 teaspoon chopped oregano
- 2 tablespoons *sofrito* (see recipe on page 13)
- ¾ cup Goya olive oil (not extra virgin)
- 8 pork chops, bone-in, about 4 ounces each
- vegetable oil for frying

Procedure:

1 Marinate the pork chops: In a bowl, combine the *adobo* with the black pepper, garlic, oregano and *sofrito*. Pour in the olive oil and mix well to form a marinade. Add the pork chops, and toss well to coat. Set aside in the refrigerator to marinate overnight.

2 In a deep fryer or skillet, heat about 3 inches of vegetable oil to 350°F. Remove the *chuletas* from the marinade and scrape any excess *sofrito* particles which may burn in the frying process. Add the chops in batches to the hot oil. Fry for about 9 minutes, keeping them submerged during the frying process, until they are crisp and a deep golden color has developed. Remove from the oil, and set aside to drain on paper towels. Serve a side of rice and beans or *tostones* (see recipe on page 47).

Although *pernil* is consumed year-round mostly in *panaderías* in the form of Cuban sandwiches, it is during the Christmas season, served alongside *Arroz con Gandules* (see recipe on page 113), when it shines the most, becoming the centerpiece at any family gathering.

Pernil

Roast Pork Butt
Serves 6 to 8

Ingredients:

- 3 tablespoons *adobo* (see recipe on page 6)
- 1 teaspoon freshly ground black pepper
- 5 tablespoons *sofrito* (see recipe on page 13)
- 8 cloves garlic, pounded to a paste, plus extra cloves
- 2 tablespoons chopped oregano
- 1 cup Goya olive oil (not extra virgin)
- one fresh pork butt, bone-in, about 6½ pounds
- ¼ cup *achiote* oil (see recipe on page 6)

Procedure:

1. Prepare the marinade: In a bowl, combine the *adobo* with the black pepper, the *sofrito*, garlic paste and oregano. Pour in the olive oil, mix well, and set aside.

2. Make small incisions along the surface of the *pernil* and stuff them with peeled garlic cloves. Rub the entire pork butt with the prepared marinade, carefully lifting the skin without tearing it, to rub some inside, and getting marinade into the incisions as well. Set aside in the refrigerator to marinate for at least 1 hour. If time allows, marinate overnight.

3. Preheat the oven to 275°F. Transfer the *pernil* to a baking rack (reserving any marinade that is left over), and place over a baking sheet. Place in the oven, and slow roast until the skin starts to crisp, about 2 hours.

4. Remove the *pernil* from the oven, and raise the oven temperature to 350°F. Brush the *pernil* with the *achiote* oil and the reserved marinade, and return to the oven for another hour, until the skin is completely crisp and the juices from the pork run clear. (If a thermometer is inserted in the thickest part of the pork butt, it should read from 170°F to 180°F). Remove the *pernil* from the oven, and set aside to rest at room temperature for about 20 minutes. Carve, and serve.

Chapter VI

Meat

Chapter VI

Meat

Bistec Empanado

Breaded Beef Tenderloin Cutlets
Serves 4

Ingredients:

- 4 beef tenderloin medallions, about 8 ounces each
- 2 tablespoons *adobo* (see recipe on page 6)
- 2 tablespoons Goya olive oil (not extra virgin)
- flour for dredging
- 6 eggs, beaten
- 10 ounces soda crackers, finely ground
- 4 ounces unsalted butter
- ½ cup vegetable oil

Procedure:

1 Pound the meat: Cut each medallion into eight 4-ounce pieces, and arrange on a clean flat surface. Using the flat side of a mallet, pound each piece of meat to a ⅛-inch thickness, (being careful not to tear the meat) and set aside.

2 Season the beef steaks: In a small bowl, combine the *adobo* with the olive oil, and mix well. Rub the beef steaks evenly with the mixture and set aside in the refrigerator to marinate for 1 hour to overnight.

3 Bread the meat: One by one, dredge the beef steaks with the flour, and shake off any excess. Dip the dredged steaks in the eggs, and bread with the ground crackers. (If you want a thicker crust, repeat the process). Set the breaded beef steaks aside.

4 In a large skillet, melt the butter with the vegetable oil, and heat up to 350°F. Add the breaded beef steaks to the hot oil, and fry for about 2 minutes. Flip and fry for another minute until golden and crisp on both sides. Remove from the oil, and set aside to drain on paper towels for about 2 minutes before serving (until the oils present in the breading recede the true crispness will not emerge).

Bistec Empanado is a staple at any local cafeteria, usually served with French fries or a side of rice and beans. This cutlet is also delicious made into a hearty sandwich or served with a fried egg on top.

Chapter VI

Meat

Empanada Parmesana

Breaded Beef Tenderloin Cutlets Parmesan

Serves 4

Ingredients:

- 4 beef tenderloin medallions, about 8 ounces each
- 2 tablespoons *adobo* (see recipe on page 6)
- 2 tablespoons Goya olive oil (not extra virgin)
- flour for dredging
- 6 eggs, beaten
- 10 ounces soda crackers, finely ground
- 4 ounces unsalted butter
- ½ cup vegetable oil
- ½ cup spaghetti sauce
- ½ cup shredded mozzarella

Although we refer to this recipe as "Parmesana" the cheese used is mozarella.

Procedure:

1 Pound the meat: Cut each medallion into eight 4-ounce pieces and arrange on a clean flat surface. Using the flat side of a mallet, pound each piece of meat to a ⅛-inch thickness (being careful not to tear the meat) and set aside.

2 Season the beef steaks: In a small bowl, combine the *adobo* with the olive oil and mix well. Rub the beef steaks evenly with the mixture and set aside in the refrigerator to marinate for at least 1 hour. If time allows, marinate overnight.

3 Bread the beef cutlets: One by one, dredge the beef steaks with the flour and shake off any excess. Dip the dredged steaks in the eggs, and bread with the ground crackers. (If you want a thicker crust on the cutlets, repeat the breading process). Set the breaded beef steaks aside.

4 In a large skillet, melt the butter with the vegetable oil, and heat up to 350° F. Add the breaded beef steaks to the hot oil, and fry for about 2 minutes. Flip and fry for another minute until golden and crisp on both sides. Remove from the oil, and set aside to drain on paper towels.

5 Preheat the oven to 350°F. Arrange the fried breaded steaks on a baking sheet with a lip. Spoon 1 tablespoon of marinara sauce over each steak, and sprinkle with 1 tablespoon of mozzarella. Place in the oven, and bake until the cheese melts, about 8 to 10 minutes. Remove from the oven, and serve with a side of *Amarillos en Almíbar* (see recipe on page 53), rice and beans, or *tostones* (see recipe on page 47).

> Chapter VI
>
> Meat

This particular cut of meat was popularized by the Argentinean community of Puerto Rico. With time, it has become the meat cut of choice at barbeques.

Churrasco

Skirt Steak
Serves 4

Ingredients:

- 1 tablespoon *adobo* (see recipe on page 6)
- ¼ teaspoon freshly ground black pepper
- 2 tablespoons *sofrito* (see recipe on page 13)
- 1 clove garlic, pounded to a paste
- 1 teaspoon chopped oregano
- ½ cup Goya olive oil (not extra virgin), plus extra
- 4 skirt steaks *(churrasco)*, ½-inch thick, about 6 ounces each

Procedure:

1 Marinate the *churrasco*: In a large bowl, combine the *adobo* with the black pepper, the *sofrito*, garlic and oregano. Pour in ½ cup of the olive oil, and mix well. Add the skirt steaks, and toss to coat well. Set aside in the refrigerator to marinate for 1 hour to overnight.

2 Remove the *churrascos* from the refrigerator, and set aside at room temperature for about 10 minutes. In a large skillet over medium-high heat, heat 4 tablespoons of olive oil until it starts to smoke. Remove the steaks from the marinade. Wipe off any excess pieces of garlic or herbs that might scorch during cooking. Add to the pan, and for a medium-done steak, cook for about 4 minutes. Flip, and cook for another for 3 to 4 minutes on the other side. Remove from the pan, and serve with a side of *tostones* (see recipe on page 47) or *Ensalada de Papa* (see recipe on page 63).

Bistec Encebollado

Beefsteak with Onions
Serves 4

The term "bistec" is the outcome of a misunderstanding. Unable to pronounce the words "beef steak", locals resorted to what sounded like the proper term.

Traditionally, this recipe is prepared with top round that is brutally pounded or passed through a tenderizing device to soften. The vinegar in the marinade was originally intended for tenderizing as well. Although I call for beef tenderloin, which hardly needs to be tenderized, I still call for a vinegar-based marinade because without that layer of flavor, the dish just wouldn't be the same.

Layering the sauce with butter in the final stage of the recipe is not completely traditional, but doing it this way has had tremendous success at Pikayo (www.pikayo.com), my flagship restaurant.

Chapter VI

Meat

Ingredients:

- 4 beef tenderloin medallions, about 8 ounces each
- ¾ cup Goya olive oil (not extra virgin), divided
- ½ cup white vinegar
- 8 cloves garlic, pounded to a paste
- 2 tablespoons *adobo* (see recipe on page 6)
- 2 onions, sliced thinly into rings
- 1 cup chicken stock
- 2 ounces cold unsalted butter

Procedure:

1. Pound the meat: Cut each medallion into eight 4-ounce pieces, and arrange on a clean flat surface. Using the flat side of a mallet, pound each piece of meat to a ⅛-inch thickness (being careful not to tear the meat) and set aside.

2. Season the beef steaks: In a small bowl, combine 1/2 cup of olive oil with the vinegar and the garlic, and mix well. Season the beef steaks evenly with the *adobo*, and add to the bowl. Toss well to coat the steaks evenly with the marinade. Arrange 4 steaks in the bottom of a deep dish, and layer half the onion rings on top. Repeat with the remaining steaks and onions, and pour the remaining marinade over. Cover, and set aside in the refrigerator to marinate for 1 hour. If time allows, marinate overnight.

3. In a large sauté pan over high heat, warm 4 tablespoons of olive oil until it starts to smoke. Remove the meat from the marinade (reserving the onions and the marinade), and add to the sauté pan in batches to sear for about 45 seconds on each side. Remove the steaks from the pan, and set aside on a platter.

4. Add the onions to the pan, and cook undisturbed for about 4 minutes until they start to brown and slightly char. Stir, and continue to cook for 3 minutes until the onions are evenly browned with scattered charred bits. Deglaze with the reserved marinade, pour in the chicken stock, and stir with a wooden spoon to scrape any browned bits from the bottom of the pan. Bring to a full boil, and cook for another minute. Remove from the heat, and stir in the cold butter to thicken the sauce. Pour the sauce with the onions over the beef steaks, and serve family style.

Bistec Encebollado is probably the most common way to serve beef in the island. With a side of white rice to soak up some of the sauce from the onions, it is simply delicious. In a hurry? Whip up a *Sándwich de Bistec* for a quick lunch. Place the *bistec* and some onions on a piece of French bread smothered with mayo. Add a crisp leaf of lettuce, some juicy tomato slices and top it off with fresh *cilantro*.

Chapter VI

Meat

Carne Frita

Fried Pork
Serves 4 to 6

In my experience, this recipe should have an advisory note attached to it; I simply cannot get enough of it. I've resorted to limiting its consumption to those weekends when an all-you-can-eat attitude surfaces and I am able to enjoy the crispy, bite-sized, well-seasoned pork chunks without limits or hesitation.

Ingredients:

For the meat:
- 2 tablespoons cornstarch
- 1 tablespoons white vinegar
- 2 cloves garlic, pounded to a paste
- 1 tablespoon *sofrito* (see recipe on page 13)
- 1 teaspoon *adobo* (see recipe on page 6)
- 1¼ pounds frying pork, cubed
- vegetable oil for frying

For the onions:
- 1 tablespoon Goya olive oil (not extra virgin)
- 1 small onion, thinly sliced
- 4 cloves garlic, pounded to a paste
- pinch of salt
- pinch of freshly ground pepper
- 1 tablespoon white vinegar

Procedure:

1 Marinate the pork: In a bowl, combine the cornstarch with the vinegar and 3 tablespoons of water and mix well to make a slurry. Add the garlic, *sofrito*, and *adobo*, and stir. Add the pork, and toss well to coat every piece. Set aside in the refrigerator to marinate for about 1 hour.

2 Prepare the onions: In a sauté pan over high heat, warm the olive oil. Add the onion and garlic, season with salt and pepper and cook, stirring, for about 2 minutes. Deglaze with the vinegar and cook until it evaporates, about 1 minute. Remove from the heat and set aside.

3 Fry the pork: In a deep fryer or a skillet, heat about 3 inches of vegetable oil to 350°F. Add the pork to the hot oil in batches, and fry until the meat is cooked through and is a deep golden color, about 7 minutes. Remove from the oil and set aside to drain on paper towels for about 3 minutes before serving. Serve topped with the onion mixture.

The cornstarch added to the marinade is a foreign element to the traditional method of making *Carne Frita*. It lends the meat a crunchier texture at a faster cooking time, ensuring some moisture is present in every bite. Traditionally, *Carne Frita* is fried longer to achieve the crispy texture, producing a drier pork product. Moist or dry, *Carne Frita* is the perfect snack to wash down with a cold beer.

Chapter VI

Meat

Picadillo

Spiced Ground Beef
Makes 2 quarts

Picadillo found its way to us via the Cuban community. Its versatility and uncomplicated nature makes it a favorite in the Puerto Rican culinary repertoire.

Ingredients:

- 3 tablespoons Goya olive oil (not extra virgin)
- 1 onion, finely diced
- 1 red Bell pepper, seeds and inner white ribbing removed, finely diced
- 8 cloves garlic, pounded to a paste
- ½ cup *sofrito* (see recipe on page 13)
- 1¾ cups Goya Spanish tomato sauce
- 2 tablespoons chopped *culantro*
- 1 tablespoon chopped oregano
- 2 tablespoons kosher salt
- 4 pounds ground beef (Sirloin)
- raisins optional

Procedure:

1. In a large sauté pan over medium-high heat, warm the olive oil. Add the onion and cook for about 2 minutes, until it loses its raw taste. Add the red pepper, garlic and *sofrito* and cook, stirring, for another 3 minutes. Stir in the tomato sauce, *culantro* and oregano; season with 2 tablespoons of salt, and cook for another minute.

2. Add the meat and cook for about 4 minutes, stirring and breaking up the beef as it cooks. Season with another tablespoon of salt and continue to cook for 20 minutes, stirring occasionally until the meat is cooked through, the liquid has evaporated and the flavors have concentrated.

Serve over hot white rice.

Chayotes Rellenos

Stuffed "Chayotes"
Serves 6

Chapter VI

Meat

Ingredients:

- 1 tablespoon salt
- 3 large *chayotes*, thoroughly washed
- 3 cups *picadillo* (see recipe on page 167)
- 3 hard-boiled eggs
- 3 eggs, beaten
- ⅓ cup raisins
- ½ cup slivered or chopped almonds
- 1 cup freshly grated *Parmigiano-Reggiano* (or substitute domestic Parmesan)

Procedure:

1 Prepare the *chayotes*: In a large pot, bring abundant water (to cover) to a boil, and add salt. Cut the *chayotes* in half lengthwise, being careful of the prickly skin, and add to the boiling water. Cook until the *chayotes* are fork-tender, about 1 hour and 45 minutes. Drain the *chayotes*, and set aside to cool.

2 Hold a *chayote* half in one hand. With a spoon, remove the white pit from the center. Spoon out the flesh, leaving a thin layer that will hold the skin intact, to make a shell. Set the flesh and shell aside. Repeat with the remaining *chayotes*.

3 Prepare the filling: Finely chop the reserved *chayote* flesh, and combine in a bowl with the *picadillo*. Finely chop the hard-boiled eggs, and add to the bowl along with the raisins and the almonds. Add the beaten eggs, season with 1 tablespoon of salt, mix well, and set aside.

4 Preheat the oven to 350°F. Arrange the *chayote* shells on a baking sheet lined with parchment paper. Distribute the *picadillo* mixture among the shells, forming a slight mound, and sprinkle generously with the *Parmigiano-Reggiano* cheese.

5 Place in the oven, and bake until the stuffed *chayotes* are cooked through and the cheese has melted enough to hold the stuffing together, 15 to 20 minutes.

The *chayote* squash variety found in Puerto Rico has a thick and spiky beige-like skin. Although the skin is not edible (it could easily choke you), it suits this recipe perfectly since it can form a strong enough shell to contain the meat stuffing. The more common variety of *chayote*, which is smaller and has a smoother light-green skin, can be substituted but, because it is softer, a shorter boiling time should be considered. The skin on this other variety is edible and easier to break so, when scooping out the shell, a thicker edge of flesh should be left so that the shell doesn't collapse and spill the stuffing during baking.

Chapter VI

Meat

Stuffed Cheese

Serves 4 to 6

Queso Relleno

I clearly remember my Grandmother Milagro's kitchen, with its blue and white floor tiles and a small table next to the refrigerator. On that table, she would have a whole Edam cheese with a small square cut out on the top and a coffee spoon next to it, for everyone who came by to remove the square top and scoop off some of the cheese in the center of the ball, until most of it was carved away.

Then, she would finish carving and fill it with meat and bake it according to the recipe. I have speeded up the process by cutting the cheese in half, hollowing both halves, filling them, and pressing them back together to form the cheese sphere.

Ingredients:

- One 5 pound wheel of Edam Cheese
- 2 cups *picadillo* (see recipe on page 167)
- 3 tablespoons raisins
- 4 tablespoons pine nuts
- 1 egg, beaten
- 1 plantain leaf

Procedure:

1. Remove the wax from the cheese, and cut the wheel in half crosswise. With a paring knife, score a 1/4-inch edge around the surface of each cheese half. Using a spoon, carefully carve out the cheese from inside the drawn-out edge, holding the circumference of the cheese with your other hand as you carve, to protect it from breaking. Set the carved cheese shells aside. (Reserve the carvings for the Cheese Balls on page 33).

2. In a bowl, combine the *picadillo* with the raisins and the pine nuts and mix well. Loosely stuff the cheese shells with the *picadillo* mixture, and pack down tightly. Brush the edges of the cheese shells with beaten egg, and distribute the remaining egg over the *picadillo* stuffing to hold it together during baking.

3. Preheat the oven to 250°F. Line the bottom of a 10" round, deep baking dish or a small *caldero* with a piece of plantain leaf. (The leaf is intended to prevent the cheese from sticking to the bottom of the dish and its oils provide flavoring to the cheese). Place one stuffed cheese shell cut-side-up in the dish. Carefully lay the other stuffed shell on top to close into a ball, resembling its original shape. Wrap in plantain leaf and place in the oven. Bake for about 20 minutes, until the cheese starts melting and spreading out. Remove from the oven and, with a rubber spatula, flatten any mounds of meat that remain. Return to the oven, and bake for another 20 minutes, until the cheese starts forming a golden edge.

4. Remove the stuffed cheese from the oven, and set aside to rest for 10 to 15 minutes. Flip onto a plate, remove the plantain leaf (it is not edible) and slice; or serve with a spoon, as you would a casserole, removing any pieces of plantain leaf.

Jamón con Piña

Ham with Pineapple Sauce
Serves 6 to 8

This recipe is inspired by my Grandmother Evelyn's traditional baked *Jamón con Piña*. Yes, it is usually done in the oven, and a huge baking ham is used, studded with cloves and dressed with thinly sliced pineapple rounds. I chose to give a stovetop alternative to the original since the possibilities for a richer sauce are enhanced in a pot and, hey, it's always fun to play around with different techniques!

Chapter VI

Meat

Ingredients:

- 2 tablespoons Goya olive oil (not extra virgin)
- one canned baking ham, about 3 pounds
- 1 teaspoon Goya cloves, plus extra
- 2 ounces unsalted butter
- 1 onion, cut into large dice
- 3 cloves garlic, cut into thin slivers
- 2 cups dry cooking sherry
- ½ cup white vinegar
- 6 cups pineapple juice
- 1 pound packed brown sugar
- 1 cup Maraschino cherries, stems removed
- 3 Goya sticks cinnamon
- 3 Goya bay leaves
- 3 tablespoons cornstarch
- 3 pounds peeled pineapple, cut into ½-inch-thick pieces

Procedure:

1 In a large heavy-bottomed pot, heat the olive oil until it starts to smoke. Carefully add the ham and sear for about 2 minutes on each side until browned. Remove the ham from the pot. Stud the surface of the ham with about a dozen cloves, scattered throughout, and set aside.

2 Add the butter to the pot and allow it to melt. Add the onion and the garlic and cook for about 5 minutes until the onions start to brown, stirring the ingredients and turning the ham occasionally so it doesn't scorch.

3 Deglaze the pan with the wine and vinegar, and cook until they start to evaporate, about 6 minutes. Pour in the pineapple juice, and add the brown sugar. Add the cherries along with the cinnamon and the bay leaves, and stir well. Place 1 teaspoon of cloves on a piece of cheesecloth. Tie the ends of the cheesecloth to form a pouch and add to the sauce. In a small bowl, combine the cornstarch with 3 tablespoons of water, and mix to make a slurry. Pour the slurry into the saucepan, and mix well. Bring the mixture to a full boil, and cook for about 8 minutes.

4 Return the ham to the pot. Add the sliced pineapple, and bring to a full boil. Reduce the heat, cover, and simmer for about 35 minutes. Remove the lid, and simmer for an additional 25 minutes, basting the ham from time to time until the sauce thickens.

5 Remove the ham from the sauce. Remove and discard the cloves. Slice the ham. Remove and discard the clove pouch and the bay leaves from the sauce. Serve the ham drizzled with the pineapple sauce and with slices of pineapple and cherries on the side.

The perfect and traditional accompaniment to this dish is a chilled Ensalada de Papa (see recipe on page 63).

Chapter VI

Meat

Carne Mechada

Stuffed Pot Roast
Serves 6 to 8

Ingredients:

- 4½ pounds beef eye round in one piece, excess fat removed
- 6 ounces *chorizo*, casings removed, crumbled
- 2 tablespoons *adobo* (see recipe on page 6)
- ⅓ cup Goya olive oil (not extra virgin)
- 3 tablespoons *sofrito* (see recipe on page 13)
- 4 cloves garlic, pounded to a paste
- 1 onion, diced
- ⅓ cup Goya green olives stuffed with *pimientos*
- 7 leaves *culantro*
- 2 cups dry cooking sherry
- 1¾ cups Goya Spanish tomato sauce
- 2 Idaho potatoes, peeled and cut into large dice
- 1 carrot, peeled and sliced into 1-inch thick pieces
- 5 quarts beef stock (see recipe page 73)

Procedure:

1 Stuff the eye round: With a puncturing device (such as a sharpening steel), make an incision through the center of the eye round. Insert the device so that it goes through the length of the meat and comes out the other end, always keeping it centered. Once the incision is made, use your fingers to widen the cavity, making sure your fingers meet in the middle when inserted through each end of the meat. Insert the *chorizo* forcefully into the cavity, and tightly pack it in with the aid of your fingers. Once the *chorizo* is compactly stuffed into the meat, season the meat by rubbing it with the *adobo*. Truss the stuffed beef with butcher's twine to ensure it keeps an even shape while cooking, and set aside.

2 Braise the meat: In a wide heavy-bottomed pot over high heat, heat the olive oil until it starts to smoke. Carefully add the eye round, and sear for about 2 minutes on each side until browned. Stir in the *sofrito*, garlic, onion, olives and *culantro*, and cook for about 3 minutes. Deglaze with the wine and cook until it starts to evaporate, about 6 minutes. Add the tomato sauce, carrot and potatoes, and pour in the beef stock. Bring to a full boil, and cook for about 10 minutes. (The liquid should cover at least two thirds of the roast in order for it to braise properly).

3 Reduce the heat, cover, and simmer for about 1½ hours. Remove the lid, and cook over a rolling simmer for an additional 2 to 2½ hours, basting and turning the meat and adding water as necessary from time to time until the meat is so soft it shreds when pricked with a fork and the sauce has reduced to a thick stew.

4 Turn off the heat, and allow to rest for about 20 minutes. Slice into 1-inch thick pieces, and serve over the sauce with a side of white rice and stewed *garbanzo* beans.

ensalada carrucho langosta
bacalao funche chillo sierra
carrucho langosta pulpo ajillo
chillo sierra camarones
langosta pulpo ajillo jueyes
camarones ensalada
jueyes bacalao funche
ensalada carrucho langosta
bacalao funche chillo sierra
carrucho langosta pulpo ajillo
chillo sierra camarones
langosta pulpo ajillo jueyes

Chapter VII

Fish & Seafood

Fish & Seafood

The paradoxes of life: I would bet, general speaking, that considering Puerto Rico's geography –an island surrounded by nature's seafood bounty– most people assume it is a large consumer of fish as its primary source of protein. Not so. It is meat –specifically beef– that dominates all statistics of protein consumption.

Island-wide, there is a certain amount of skepticism when it comes to preparing fish. Most of it sprouts from what seems to be the same doubts affecting other cultures: that is, a fear based on a presumed inadequate culinary knowledge of fish and its possibilities.

In my opinion, that is one of the things that shape a culture's cuisine. When there is no knowledge, or the lack of it promotes fear, then it's time to go for the one cooking method that is most reassuring: Fry it to its crispiest point and at least you will know that the possibility of failing to make sure it's fully cooked can be disregarded. Simultaneously, you will have canceled any uncertainties regarding the growth of bacteria and subsequent illness.

To spin another layer of cultural development on the positive side, let's add some of those cooking methods and products that have been used almost daily for as long as I can remember. Take, for instance, the use of salted cod, inherited from the Spanish culture. Every Friday, in any down-home *fonda*, there has to be *Serenata de Bacalao* or it is simply not authentic. When Friday is around the corner, I almost feel like one of Pavlov's dogs, my taste buds watering for *Serenata*.

Like any other culture, we have had our own share of food-preserving challenges, pushing us and them to evolve into what today are our classical forms of food preparation. More culinary-advanced cultures have used preserving techniques such as confit, pickling, smoking, dry-curing and the like, in an effort to preserve food resources. Adaptable to all cultures, those preserving efforts are sometimes the pillars that help shape our regional palates to become the roots and foundations of our culinary heritage.

Escabeche, a favored preparation locally, both for its preserving abilities and for the distinct delicious flavor it imparts, is one that has undergone its own evolutionary process. While it is slightly away from its original recipe, it is one of those pillars.

My childhood memories when it comes to fish are those of a *colmadito*, or small grocery store, where I would always see large glass jars filled with previously fried *sierra* steaks (Kingfish) preserved in *escabeche*. Being that Puerto Rico is a largely Catholic culture, the observance of Holy Week marked the use of some of these recipes at home. Essentially, once the holidays had passed, the recipes were left in the card index until the following year's observance.

The other fish that has remained a constant staple, at least in my experiences past and present, is *Chillo Frito* or fried Red Snapper, with

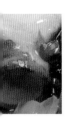

(continued)

Mojito (not to be confused with the popular Cuban rum-based cocktail). The only fish or seafood sauce that I am aware of, that is always used for fish recipes, is *Mojito*, which is nothing more than a tomato-based Creole sauce with lots of capers, olives, garlic and *cilantro*.

Whole *Chillo Frito* has always been part of the menu at Pikayo (www.pikayo.com) restaurant, and it will remain there as a classic to enjoy and one that makes me feel I have a responsibility in the preservation of our culinary traditions.

If you noticed that this is probably one of the chapters that contains the least amount of recipes in comparison to the others, that is because anywhere you go in Puerto Rico, the options for fish offered in our traditional seaside restaurants, and even those in the cities that want to portray a traditional Puerto Rican fish menu, will feature essentially three preparations: buttered, *al ajillo* (garlic butter) or *al mojito isleño*, and once those three sauces are present the rest is about which fish is fresh and available.

There are a few fish in our coastal waters that are most often seen on menus. This list will have some variations depending on the exact location of the restaurant and the time of the year. Around November, it's time for *Dorado*, known in Hawaii as Mahi Mahi and not to be confused with Spanish *Dorada* or Chilean Dorad. This is one particular species, which really grew in popularity in the 1960s and '70s. The fishing villages and coastal towns, I'm sure, knew about it and consumed it but commercially it was not very well known.

The most popular species are *Mero* (Grouper) in all of its categories and *Chillo* (Red Snapper) as well. Then you have *Cotorro* (Parrot fish), *Capitán* (Captain fish), *Colirrubia* (Yellowtail Snapper) and Marlin among those most commonly seen on menus. Another one of those fish species well known to fishermen but perhaps not the restaurant community at large is *Peto*, or Wahoo. Swordfish, taken off coastal waters, is more common these days.

Too much of the fish consumed here is imported from all over the world. Some are species that are not natural to our surrounding waters; others are simply imported for size, consistency, or flow of goods logistics. For whatever reasons, that is just the way it is! Now you know why I used the word paradox in the first sentence of this chapter.

Ensalada de Carrucho

Conch Salad
Serves 6 to 8

I had my first encounter with fresh conch back in '94 on a weekend trip to Culebra, an island adjacent to Puerto Rico. A cocky young chef, I was set on proving that I knew how to handle this ocean delicacy. Little did I know about the intensive and gross task that skinning fresh *carrucho* entailed; Ajax and hours of hard scrubbing were not enough to rid my hands of the slimy and sticky conch mucus. Lesson learned, I advise purchasing frozen or, if available, fresh conch that has been previously cleaned.

> Chapter VII
>
> Fish & Seafood

Ingredients:

- 2½ pounds cleaned conch, cut into large dice
- salt
- 1 cup vegetable oil
- 1 cup Goya olive oil (not extra virgin)
- ½ cup white vinegar
- 1 cup fresh lime juice
- 4 cloves garlic, pounded to a paste
- 1 teaspoon *pique* (see recipe on page 11) (or substitute Tabasco)
- 2 tablespoons *adobo* (see recipe on page 6)
- 1 teaspoon freshly ground black pepper
- 2 tablespoons chopped oregano
- 1 large onion, diced
- 2 cubanelle peppers, seeds and inner white ribbing removed, diced
- 1 red Bell pepper, seeds and inner white ribbing removed, diced
- ½ cup Goya olives stuffed with *pimientos*, roughly chopped
- 2 tablespoons Goya capers

Procedure:

1 Prepare the conch: Bring a pot of abundant water to a boil, and add ¼ cup of salt for every gallon of water. Add the conch to the boiling water, and blanch for about 50 seconds. Quickly drain, and transfer the conch to a bath of ice water to stop the cooking. Drain, and set aside.

2 Prepare the salad: In a bowl, combine the vegetable oil with the olive oil, vinegar, lime juice, garlic, *pique, adobo,* black pepper, and oregano. Mix well, and set aside. In a separate bowl, combine the onion with the cubanelle and red peppers, the olives, capers and conch. Pour the oil mixture over, and toss to coat well. Set the salad aside in the refrigerator to marinate overnight. Remove from the refrigerator and serve lightly chilled.

Carrucho can be tenderized by boiling it for a prolonged period of time. The end product might seem soft, yet flavorless, since the natural flavors of the conch are given away to the cooking liquid which will later be discarded. Quickly blanching and shocking the conch, as I suggest, guarantees a tender bite while preserving the conch's flavor.

Ensalada de Pulpo

Octopus Salad
Serves 6 to 8

If you are taking a road trip along the island's coast, make sure to stop by a road stand or a *colmadito* and order an octopus salad. It is customary and charmingly folkloric to find it served in paper cones or plastic cups.

Chapter VII

Fish & Seafood

Ingredients:

- one frozen Spanish or Portuguese octopus*, about 6 pounds
- 1 cup vegetable oil
- 1 cup Goya olive oil (not extra virgin)
- ½ cup white vinegar
- 1 cup fresh lime juice
- 4 cloves garlic, pounded to a paste
- 1 teaspoon *pique* (see recipe on page 11) (or substitute Tabasco)
- 2 tablespoons *adobo* (see recipe on page 6)
- 1 teaspoon freshly ground black pepper
- 2 tablespoons chopped oregano
- 1 large onion, diced
- 2 cubanelle peppers, seeds and inner white ribbing removed, diced
- 1 red Bell pepper, seeds and inner white ribbings removed, diced
- ½ cup Goya olives stuffed with *pimientos*, roughly chopped
- 2 tablespoons Goya capers

Procedure:

1 Cook the octopus: Bring a large pot of abundant water to a boil. Completely submerge the octopus in the boiling water. Return to a full boil, and cook for 30 minutes. Turn off the heat, cover with a tight-fitting lid, and set aside undisturbed for 10 minutes. Drain, and transfer the octopus to a bath of ice water to stop the cooking. Drain, and set aside.

2 Slice the octopus: Using a knife or a pair of scissors, cut out and discard the head from the base of the tentacles. Separate the tentacles from the base, and set aside. Slice the base into ¼-inch-thick pieces, and set aside. Cut away and discard any gummy or fatty excesses on the tentacles. (If you prefer, cut away the suckers from the tentacles). Slice the tentacles into ¼-inch-thick pieces, and set aside.

3 Prepare the salad: In a bowl, combine the vegetable oil with the olive oil, vinegar, lime juice, garlic, *pique, adobo*, black pepper, and oregano. Mix well, and set aside. In a separate bowl, combine the onion with the cubanelle and red peppers, the olives, capers and the sliced octopus. Pour the oil mixture over, and toss to coat well. Set the salad aside in the refrigerator to marinate overnight. Remove from the refrigerator and serve chilled.

*Spanish or Portuguese octopus is of a far better quality and tends to be most tender, shortening the time it takes to boil and soften. A six-pound octopus might seem like a lot to the average cook, yet when preparing octopus, the shrinkage factor during boiling and the fact that it will be freed of fatty and unwanted tissue should be taken into account.

Chapter VII

Fish & Seafood

Camarones al Ajillo

Shrimp in Garlic Sauce

Serves 4

Ingredients:

For the sauce:
- 1 pound cold butter, cut into small pieces
- 30 cloves garlic, cut into thin slivers
- ¼ cup white vinegar
- 1 cup dry Spanish sherry
- 2 teaspoons salt
- 3 tablespoons chopped *culantro*

For the shrimp:
- 3 tablespoons butter
- 1 tablespoon Goya olive oil (not extra virgin)
- 20 jumbo shrimp, peeled and deveined, tails left intact
- 1 tablespoon salt
- freshly ground black pepper

Procedure:

1 Prepare the garlic sauce: In a sauté pan over medium-high heat, melt 4 ounces of butter. Add the garlic slivers and cook for about 2 minutes, stirring and shaking the pan so that the garlic does not stick to the bottom of the pan and no browning occurs. Deglaze with the sherry and the vinegar, season with the salt and add the *culantro*. Cook until the liquid starts to boil and reduce, 4 to 6 minutes. At this point, lower the heat and stir in the remaining pieces of cold butter. When the butter has almost completely melted and smoothed out the sauce, remove the pan from the heat and continue stirring until the butter completely melts, forming a sauce thick enough to coat the back of a spoon.

2 Cook the shrimp: In a sauté pan over high heat, melt the butter with the olive oil. Season the shrimp with salt and pepper and add to the pan. Cook for about 2 minutes on each side; remove from the heat. Add to the garlic sauce, toss well, and serve.

Chapter VII

Fish & Seafood

Langosta al Ajillo

Providing an alternative to our classic garlic sauce, which consists of melted butter, I included this take on *beurre blanc*, with the addition of garlic.

Lobster with Garlic Sauce

Serves 4

Ingredients:

For the lobster:
- 4 lobster tails, shelled, about 6 ounces each
- 1 teaspoon salt
- freshly ground black pepper
- 8 tablespoons butter

For the sauce:
- 1 pound cold butter, cut into small pieces
- 30 cloves garlic, cut into thin slivers
- ¼ cup white vinegar
- 1 cup dry Spanish sherry
- 2 teaspoons salt
- 3 tablespoons chopped *culantro*

Procedure:

1 Cook the lobster: Preheat the oven to 350°F. Season the lobster tails with salt and pepper and arrange in a flat baking pan with a slight lip. Distribute the butter over the lobster and place in the oven. Bake for about 20 minutes or until cooked through and tender.

2 Meanwhile, prepare the garlic sauce: In a sauté pan over medium-high heat, melt 4 ounces of butter. Add the garlic slivers and cook for about 2 minutes, stirring and shaking the pan so that the garlic does not stick to the bottom of the pan and no browning occurs. Deglaze with the sherry and the vinegar, season with the salt and add the *culantro*. Cook until the liquid starts to boil and reduce, 4 to 6 minutes. At this point, lower the heat and stir in the remaining pieces of cold butter. When the butter has almost completely melted and smoothed out the sauce, remove the pan from the heat and continue stirring until the butter completely melts, forming a sauce thick enough to coat the back of a spoon.

3 Remove the lobster from the oven and serve drizzled with the garlic sauce.

Chapter VII

Fish & Seafood

The authenticity of *salmorejo* depends on the use of *jueyes*, or Puerto Rican land crabs. These crabs are fed a corn-based diet, resulting in a slightly different flavor from their blue-crab counterparts.

Salmorejo de Jueyes

Crab Meat "Salmorejo"

Serves 4 to 6

Ingredients:

- 3 tablespoons Goya olive oil (not extra virgin)
- 2 tablespoons *achiote* oil (see recipe on page 6)
- 3 ounces *tocino*, cut into fine dice
- ½ onion, cut into fine dice
- ½ cubanelle pepper, seeds and inner white ribbings removed, cut into fine dice
- 8 cloves garlic, pounded to a paste
- ¼ cup *sofrito* (see recipe on page 13)
- 1 cup Goya Spanish tomato sauce
- 2 tablespoons Goya capers
- 1 pound *jueyes* meat (or substitute blue crab claw meat)
- ½ teaspoons kosher salt
- 2 tablespoons chopped *culantro*

Procedure:

1. In a large sauté pan over high heat, warm the olive oil with the *achiote* oil. Add the *tocino* and cook for about 3 minutes, until it starts rendering its fat and melting away. Add the onion, pepper, garlic and *sofrito* and cook, stirring until the onion is soft and loses its raw taste, about 3 minutes. Add the tomato sauce and capers and cook for another 2 minutes, stirring so the sauce does not stick to the bottom of the pan. Stir in the crab meat, season with the salt and cook for another 2 minutes. Stir in the *culantro* and remove from the heat.

Salmorejo de Jueyes goes a long way when transformed into other dishes. *Arroz con Jueyes* (see recipe on page 117), for example, takes it to another level; the addition of eggs, fresh bread crumbs and other seasonings turn a simple *salmorejo* into *criollo* crab cakes, and in my signature restaurant, Pikayo (www.pikayo.com), we have a modern application for the traditional recipe. The *salmorejo* is sautéed with a dash of *pique* and some heavy cream, and tossed with spaghetti or *fettuccine*.

Serenata de Bacalao

Salt Cod Salad with Root Vegetables
Serves 4 to 6

There are as many ways to prepare *serenata* as there are ripples in the ocean from Spain to Puerto Rico. My contribution celebrates an old countryside tradition, which involves dredging and frying the *bacalao* prior to making the salad. This light coating provides a fundamental element because it helps the fish absorb the flavors from the dressing.

Chapter VII

Fish & Seafood

Ingredients:

- 1½ pounds premium salt cod fillet
- 2 cups milk
- flour for dredging
- vegetable oil for frying
- salt
- 8 ounces *ñame*, peeled and cut into ½-inch dice
- 8 ounces *apio*, peeled and cut into ½-inch dice
- 8 ounces *yautía*, peeled and cut into ½-inch dice
- ¾ cup Goya olive oil (not extra virgin)
- ¼ cup white vinegar
- 3 tablespoons *culantro*
- ½ small onion, julienned
- 3 hard-boiled eggs, cut into wedges
- 5 plum tomatoes, seeds removed, cut into fine dice
- Romaine lettuce leaves for garnish

Procedure:

1 Reconstitute the salt cod: Place the salt cod in a deep dish and cover with the milk and 2 cups of water. Cover and set aside in the refrigerator to soak overnight. The milk acts as a tenderizer for a silkier texture and a more tender bite.

2 Prepare the root vegetables: Bring a pot of abundant water to a boil. Add salt and the *ñame, apio* and *yautía* and cook until fork-tender, about 10 minutes. Drain the root vegetables and set aside to cool.

3 Meanwhile, drain the salt cod and carefully remove any small bones or tough skin that remains. Cut the fillet into cubes and set aside. In a deep fryer or skillet, heat about 3 inches of vegetable oil to 350°F. Dredge the salt cod cubes in flour, shake off any excess, and carefully lower into the hot oil. Fry until golden and crisp, about 4 minutes. Remove from the oil and set aside to drain on paper towels.

4 Prepare the *serenata:* In a small bowl, combine the olive oil with the vinegar and the *cilantro*, mix well, and set aside. In a separate bowl, combine the root vegetables with the onion and the fried salt cod. Pour the oil mixture over, and toss like you would a salad. Set aside in the refrigerator to marinate for at least 1 hour. If time allows, marinate overnight. Carefully correct the seasoning, if necessary, with the salt since there is a great amount of salt in the cod to begin with.

5 To serve, remove the *serenata* from the refrigerator, allowing it to come to room temperature (the root vegetables get a bit hard when refrigerated). Arrange a lettuce leaf on a plate and spoon some *serenata* on top. Place a couple of hard-boiled egg wedges on the side and scatter the diced tomatoes on top.

Chapter VII

Fish & Seafood

Bacalao *a la Vizcaína*

Baked Salt Cod Stew with Potatoes

Serves 4 to 6

Ingredients:

- 1½ pounds premium salt-cod fillet
- 2 cups milk
- 3 tablespoons Goya olive oil (not extra virgin), plus extra
- 1 large onion, thinly sliced
- 4 cloves garlic, pounded to a paste
- 2 tablespoons *sofrito* (see recipe on page 13)
- ⅛ cup white vinegar
- 1 ¾ cups Goya Spanish tomato sauce
- 3 tablespoons sugar
- ¼ cup Goya green olives stuffed with *pimientos*
- ¼ cup raisins
- 3 tablespoons chopped *culantro*
- 2 Idaho potatoes, peeled and sliced into ⅛-inch-thick pieces

Procedure:

1 Reconstitute the salt cod: Place the salt cod in a deep dish and cover with the milk and 2 cups of water. Cover, and set aside in the refrigerator to soak overnight. The milk acts as a tenderizer for a silkier texture and a more tender bite.

2 Drain the salt cod, and carefully remove any small bones or tough skin that remains. Slice the salt cod, coarsely chop, and set aside

3 In a straight-sided ovenproof skillet, warm 3 tablespoons of olive oil. Add the onion, garlic and *sofrito*, and cook until the onion is translucent and loses its raw taste, about 4 minutes. Deglaze with the vinegar and cook until it starts to evaporate, about 1 minute. Stir in the salt cod; add the tomato sauce. Sprinkle with the sugar, and stir. Add the olives, raisins and *culantro* and cook, stirring to obtain a thick stew, about 5 minutes.

4 Preheat the oven to 350°F. Arrange the potatoes shingled in a circular pattern over the stew. Drizzle with olive oil and cook until the stew starts to bubble in between the potatoes, another 3 minutes. Transfer to the oven and bake until the flavors of the stew are well concentrated and the potatoes start to crisp and turn golden, about 20 minutes.

Chapter VII

Fish & Seafood

Most every culture has a cornmeal-based recipe tradition. In Puerto Rico, it is mostly used for making *sorullos*. *Funche*, on the other hand, is a deep-rooted traditional recipe that might be slowly becoming extinct. It was considered a breakfast of champions to *campesinos* (country men) who consumed the dish early in the morning to fuel up for the day's chores.

Funche con Bacalao

Salt Cod Polenta

Serves 6

Ingredients:

- 1¼ pounds premium salt cod fillet
- 2 cups whole milk
- 8 ounces butter
- 4 cloves garlic, pounded to a paste
- 1 small onion, cut into fine dice
- 2 tablespoons *sofrito* (see recipe on page 13)
- 5 cups chicken stock (see recipe on page 72)
- 2 cups Goya coconut milk
- 1 tablespoon finely chopped oregano
- 2 tablespoons sugar
- 2½ cups fine cornmeal
- 2 tablespoons finely chopped *culantro*

Procedure:

1. Reconstitute the salt cod: Place the salt cod in a deep dish and cover with the milk and 2 cups of water. Cover and set aside in the refrigerator to soak overnight. The milk acts as a tenderizer for a silkier texture and a more tender bite.

2. Drain the salt cod, and carefully remove any small bones or tough skin that remains. Slice the salt-cod, coarsely chop, and set aside.

3. In a large saucepan over high heat, melt the butter. Add the garlic, onion and *sofrito* and cook, stirring until the onion is soft and loses its raw taste, about 3 minutes. Add the chicken stock, coconut milk, oregano and sugar. Bring to a full boil.

4. Slowly pour in the cornmeal and stir rapidly with a wooden spoon to form a creamy pasty mixture. Continue to cook for about 5 minutes over high heat, as you stir. When the mixture starts bubbling, add the *bacalao* and continue to cook, stirring, for 2 minutes until it starts to separate from the corners of the saucepan Stir in the *culantro* and remove from the heat. Serve hot.

Chapter VII

Fish & Seafood

Revoltillo con Bacalao

Scrambled Eggs with Salt Cod

Serves 4 to 6

Ingredients:

- ½ pound premium salt cod fillet
- 1 cup milk
- 12 eggs
- 1 cup heavy cream
- 4 tablespoons butter
- 1 small onion, cut into fine dice
- 4 ounces cream cheese, cut into small chunks
- ⅓ cup chopped chives
- 1 tablespoon chopped *cilantro*

Procedure:

1 Reconstitute the salt cod: Place the salt cod in a deep dish and cover with the milk and 1 cup of water. Cover, and set aside in the refrigerator to soak overnight. The milk acts as a tenderizer for a silkier texture and a more tender bite.

2 Drain the salt cod and carefully remove any small bones or tough skin that remains. Slice the salt cod, coarsely chop, and set aside.

3 Prepare the eggs: Crack the eggs into a bowl with the heavy cream and beat until smooth. Set aside. In a large saucepan over high heat, melt the butter. Add the onion and cook, stirring until it starts to brown, about 4 minutes. Add the beaten eggs to the pan and cook for about 2 minutes, stirring and scraping the eggs from the bottom of the pan with a rubber spatula as they cook.

4 Add the salt cod to the eggs and continue to cook, stirring and scraping, for another 4 minutes. Incorporate the cream cheese into the eggs (which at this point should still be on the wet side), and cook, stirring until the cheese melts into the scrambled eggs, another 3 minutes. Stir in the chives and the *cilantro* and remove from the heat. Serve hot. (If drier scrambled eggs are desired, cook further).

Aside from being a great breakfast dish, *Revoltillo con Bacalao* is commonly served as a lunch item in *fondas* or local diners, with a generous side of white rice and red beans.

Chapter VII
Fish & Seafood

Sierra en Escabeche

Pickled Kingfish
Serves 6

Ingredients:

For the fish:
- 6 Kingfish steaks, about 8 ounces each
- 2 tablespoons *adobo* (see recipe on page 6)
- vegetable oil for frying

For the *escabeche*:
- 8 cups Goya olive oil (not extra virgin)
- 3 large onions, julienned
- 2 tablespoons *adobo* (see recipe on page 6)
- 1 tablespoon black peppercorns
- 20 Goya bay leaves
- ½ cup Goya green olives stuffed with *pimientos*
- 2 cups white vinegar

Procedure:

1 Fry the fish: In a deep fryer or a skillet, heat about 3 inches of vegetable oil to 350°F. Season the Kingfish steaks with the *adobo* and add in batches to the hot oil. Fry until the fish is cooked through and is a golden brown, 3 to 4 minutes. Remove from the oil and set aside to drain on paper towels.

2 Prepare the *escabeche*: In a large skillet over medium-high heat, warm ½ cup of the olive oil. Add the onions, season with 1 tablespoon of *adobo* and cook, stirring so no browning occurs, until the onions start to wilt and lose their raw flavor, about 5 minutes. Add the vinegar, peppercorns and olives and cook for another 2 minutes.

3 Add the remaining olive oil and the bay leaves, stir carefully, and lower the heat. Cook for another 5 minutes so that the herbs and spices flavor the oil. Remove from the heat and set aside to cool to room temperature.

4 Place the *sierra* steaks into a large glass jar, being careful not to break them, and pour the *escabeche* in to cover the fish. Tightly seal the jar and set aside to steep in the refrigerator for up to 1 week. Allow to rest at room temperature before serving.

Because *escabeche* was originally prepared as a way to preserve ingredients, it is not intended for refrigeration. Nonetheless, refrigerating the *escabeche* will achieve the same results with a far lower risk of food-borne illnesses.

When I think of *Sierra en Escabeche*, a childhood imprint always comes to mind: I am immediately transported to one Easter holiday, passing through a *colmadito* in the town of Cayey where glass jars, packed with heart-shaped *sierra* steaks, bay leaves, peppercorns and oil, rested on the counter for a quick grab.

This particular recipe prevails throughout the island, particularly during Easter and Lent. The pickled fish is so delicious that the promise to abstain from eating meat seems more like a blessing than a sacrifice.

Chapter VII

Fish & Seafood

Chillo Frito

Fried Red Snapper

Serves 1 to 2

Ingredients:

- 1 whole Red Snapper, dressed (scaled and gutted), 1½ to 2¼ pounds
- 2 teaspoons *adobo* (see recipe on page 6)
- flour for dredging
- vegetable oil for frying
- lime wedges

See step-by-step procedure on page 236

Fried whole fish is very popular throughout the island's coasts. It is usually served flat on its side on an elongated plate, causing the crispness to dwindle by the time the fish is turned over. Standing the fish during frying, and serving it likewise, ensures that the whole fish will remain crisp. Scoring the flesh of the fish not only provides for extra crunch, but guarantees an almost bone-free eating experience.

Procedure:

1 Score the fish: Lay the Red Snapper on its side. With a sharp knife, score the fish diagonally along its surface at 1-inch intervals, reaching all the way to the central bone. Turn the fish around, and score once more across the original incisions, to form 1-inch squares along the surface of the fish. Turn the fish over, and repeat the scoring on the other side.

2 Season both sides of the fish with the *adobo*, making sure all the crevices are well seasoned. Dredge the fish in flour and shake off any excess.

3 Stand the dredged fish on its belly and fold into a horseshoe shape, so its mouth meets the tail. Thread the folded fish with a wooden skewer to hold its shape, and set aside.

4 In a stock pot or deep fryer, heat to 350°F enough vegetable oil to cover the fish. Using tongs, carefully lower the fish into the hot oil, belly-down, and fry undisturbed, until it is crisp and a deep golden color, about 10 minutes.

5 Carefully remove the fish from the oil and set aside to drain on paper towels. Serve the fish standing on its belly, with some lime wedges on the side to squeeze over it, and *salsa criolla* (see recipe on page 12) for dipping.

ieso pan **budín guayaba**
flan coco lechoza **arroz con du**
udín **guayaba** pastelillos te
hoza **arroz con dulce vainilla**
yaba pastelillos **tembleque**
z **con dulce vainilla queso** pa
pastelillos **tembleque flan** co
ce **vainilla queso** pan **budín**
leque **flan** coco lechoza **arro**
ieso pan **budín guayaba**
flan coco lechoza **arroz con du**
udín **guayaba** pastelillos te

Chapter VIII

Desserts

Desserts

Our desserts are simply reflections of what was available back when we did not have access to what the rest of the world had to offer. Such is not the case at present. Today, overnight shipping can furnish beautiful fresh fruits and everything else under the sun immediately, if you are willing to pay the price.

But the unofficial, all time favorite dessert in Puerto Rico remains *Flan*, in any of its most popular flavors: vanilla, coconut and in recent decades, cheese. Even the most basic *fonda* or the most complex restaurant prepare some form of *flan* to please the local palate as well as that of visitors.

In terms of culinary adoption, there are desserts that are consumed here daily, such as *Tres Leches*, which is nothing more than sponge cake soaked in a combination of condensed, evaporated and fresh milk. But despite its popularity, it is not ours to claim as a part of our early culture.

The presence of fruits in our dessert menu is all due to the abundance of them locally. Candied Guava Shells with Farmers Cheese is a huge favorite, but almost never available fresh, so most of it is canned. The best Farmer's Cheese, in my opinion, is *Queso de Hoja*, which translates to "leaf cheese", and gets its name from the very many thin layers of cheese that compose the final piece. *Queso de Hoja* is hard to get, at least in the form that I remember this cheese when Grandpa William presented it to me, since it is very artisanal and, as in any culture, the artisans are disappearing.

Candied fruits and compotes, or *Dulces*, which translates literally to "sweets", are very common and made from orange skins, passion fruit skins, green papayas, mangoes, *grosellas* and even some roots like sweet potatoes. Made to a candy state, they are then wrapped in dry plantain leafs, offering exotic flavors even for locals.

When and how puff pastry arrived to our land is uncertain to me, but we love puff pastry in many ways.

The breakfast period is a witness to a very popular dessert-like specialty called *quesitos*, which translates to "little cheese". These are consumed for breakfast principally but are available all day, and they are nothing more that puff pastry rolled like a cylinder the size of a large cigar, and filled with sugared cream cheese. The other puff pastry dessert / sweet snack is *Pastelillos de Guayaba*, which are puff pastry squares baked hollow and filled with guava paste and dusted with powdered sugar. These are served at birthday parties for kids or adults, when local treats are desired.

Rice pudding and coconut pudding are two classic desserts that are mostly used during the Christmas season, although you occasionally see them throughout the year.

The use of cloves, cinnamon, star anise, vanilla, ginger, exotic fruits and dairy products are evident throughout our desserts, providing for easy, rustic, yet very intense and delicious desserts which clearly reflect our simple styles.

203

Chapter VIII

Desserts

Dulce de Lechosa

Candied Papaya

Serves 6 to 8

The pinnacle factor in the success of this recipe is that the papaya be green. A ripe papaya will result in a soft candy that falls apart. Green papaya, on the other hand, will absorb the flavors of the syrup and keep firm throughout the cooking process.

Ingredients:

- 1 green papaya, about 3 pounds
- 8 pods star anise
- 2 tablespoons Goya cloves
- 3 cups sugar
- 6 Goya cinnamon sticks
- 1 teaspoon baking soda

Procedure:

1 Peel the papaya. Slice it in half lengthwise and, with a spoon, remove and discard the seeds (or reserve and grind to use in salad dressings). Slice the papaya into ¼-inch thick wedges and place in a heavy-bottomed pot. Place the anise pods and the cloves on a piece of cheesecloth. Tie the edges of the cheesecloth to make a pouch and add to the pot, along with the sugar, cinnamon sticks and baking soda. Pour in 1 ½ cups of water and bring to a full boil over high heat.

2 Lower the heat and simmer for about 45 minutes, until the papaya slices are tender with a firm bite and the syrup has reduced. Remove from the heat and set aside to cool. Refrigerate overnight before serving.

Traditionally, candied papaya is served with sliced *queso fresco del país* which is bland enough to contrast with the sweetness of the candied fruit.

Chapter VIII

Desserts

Flan de Coco

Coconut Custard

Serves 8 to 10

Ingredients:

For the caramel:
- 1 cup sugar
- 1 cup water

For the custard:
- one 12-ounce can condensed milk
- two 12-ounce cans evaporated milk
- one 15-ounce can Goya coconut cream
- 12 eggs, beaten
- 1 15-ounce can Goya coconut milk *(leche de coco)*

Procedure:

Preheat the oven to 300°F.

1 Prepare the caramel: In a small saucepan over high heat, combine the water and the sugar. Bring to a boil and cook for 13 minutes, until a deep golden caramel has formed. Remove from the heat and immediately pour into a 9" round ceramic baking dish, so that it covers the bottom. Set aside for the caramel to harden.

2 Prepare the custard: In a bowl, combine the evaporated milk with the condensed milk, coconut cream, coconut milk, and the eggs and whisk until smooth. Pour the custard mixture into the prepared baking dish.

3 Place the baking dish into a larger baking pan and place in the oven. Pour enough water into the outer baking pan to make a water bath *(baño de maría)* that covers about three quarters of the baking dish containing the flan.

4 Bake for about 1 hour until the custard starts to set. Carefully remove from the oven. Remove the custard from the water bath and set aside to cool for about 20 minutes. Set aside in the refrigerator to set overnight.

5 To serve, flip the flan onto a serving platter (at this point, the caramel should be liquid). Slice and serve.

Flan de Queso

Cheese Custard

Serves 6 to 8

Ingredients:

For the caramel:
- 1 cup sugar
- 1 cup water

For the custard:
- 24 ounces cream cheese
- 1½ cups sugar
- 8 eggs
- 2 cups heavy cream
- 2 cups whole milk

Procedure:

Preheat the oven to 300°F.

1. Prepare the caramel: In a small saucepan over high heat, combine the water and the sugar. Bring to a boil and cook for 13 minutes, until a deep golden caramel has formed. Remove from the heat and immediately pour into a 9" round ceramic baking dish, so that it covers the bottom. Set aside for the caramel to harden.

2. Prepare the custard: In a standing mixer, combine the cream cheese and sugar, and beat on medium speed for about 2 minutes. Add the eggs and continue to beat until the mixture is soft and free of lumps, another 4 minutes. Add the heavy cream and the milk and beat for another minute until well incorporated. Pour the custard mixture into the prepared baking pan.

3. Place the baking dish into a larger baking pan and place in the oven. Pour enough water into the outer baking pan to make a water bath *(baño de maría)* that covers about three quarters of the baking dish containing the *flan*.

4. Bake for about 1 hour until the custard starts to set. Carefully remove from the oven. Remove the custard from the water bath and set aside to cool for about 20 minutes. Set aside in the refrigerator to set overnight.

5. To serve, flip the *flan* onto a serving platter (at this point, the caramel should be liquid). Slice and serve.

Chapter VIII

Desserts

Flan de Vainilla

Vanilla Custard

Serves 8 to 10

Ingredients:

For the caramel:
- 1 cup sugar
- 1 cup water

For the custard:
- two 12-ounce cans condensed milk
- one 12-ounce can evaporated milk
- 8 eggs, beaten
- 1 tablespoon vanilla extract
- ⅛ teaspoon kosher salt

Procedure:

Preheat the oven to 300°F.

1 Prepare the caramel: In a small saucepan over high heat, combine the water and the sugar. Bring to a boil and cook for 13 minutes, until a deep golden caramel has formed. Remove from the heat and immediately pour into a 9" round ceramic baking dish, so that it covers the bottom. Set aside for the caramel to harden.

2 Prepare the custard: In a bowl, combine the condensed milk with the evaporated milk, eggs and vanilla extract. Add the salt and whisk until smooth. Pour the custard mixture into the prepared baking dish.

3 Place the baking dish into a larger baking pan and place in the oven. Pour enough water into the outer baking pan to make a water bath *(baño de maría)* that covers about three quarters of the baking dish containing the *flan*.

4 Bake for about 1 hour until the custard starts to set. Carefully remove from the oven. Remove the custard from the water bath and set aside to cool for about 20 minutes. Set aside in the refrigerator to set overnight.

5 To serve, flip the *flan* onto a serving platter (at this point, the caramel should be liquid). Slice and serve.

Desserts
Chapter VIII

Budín de Pan

Bread Pudding
Serves 6 to 8

Ingredients:

- 6 whole eggs, plus 6 egg yolks
- 1¾ cups sugar
- 3 cups whole milk
- 2 cups heavy cream
- 1 tablespoon vanilla extract
- 1 pound French baguette
- ½ cup raisins

Procedure:

1 In a large bowl, combine the eggs and egg yolks with the sugar and beat until soft and creamy. Add the milk, heavy cream and vanilla extract. With a whisk, mix until the ingredients are well incorporated. Set aside.

2 With a serrated knife, cut the baguette into 1-inch cubes and add to the bowl with the cream mixture along with the raisins. Toss well to completely coat the pieces of bread. Set aside in the refrigerator to soak overnight.

3 Preheat the oven to 350°F. Remove the bread mixture from the refrigerator and stir to make sure all the bread is completely wet. Line the bottom of a 9" round mold with parchment paper and pour in the bread mixture. Shake the mold so that the mixture settles evenly. Place in the oven. Bake for about 45 minutes until the pudding sets. Remove from the oven and set aside to cool before serving.

Croissants, although not pertaining to our culture, would greatly enhance this recipe when substituted for the French bread which is traditionally used. Although both belong to the French culture, the additional butter content and airiness of croissants provide for a special spongy effect not obtainable with French bread.

Chapter VIII

Desserts

Arroz con Dulce

Rice Pudding
Serves 8 to 10

Ingredients:

- 4 Goya cinnamon sticks
- 4 tablespoons of grated fresh ginger
- ¼ cup Goya cloves
- two 12-ounce cans evaporated milk
- 2 cups whole milk
- 1 cup raisins
- 3 cups medium-grain rice, soaked in water overnight, drained
- two 15-ounce cans Goya coconut cream
- Goya ground cinnamon for dusting

Procedure:

1 In a saucepan, combine 5 cups of water with the cinnamon sticks, ginger root and cloves. Bring to a full boil and cook for about 7 minutes. Pass through a colander and set the strained liquid aside.

2 In a heavy-bottomed pot over high heat, combine the flavored liquid with the evaporated milk, the whole milk and the raisins. Bring to a full boil. Add the rice and return to a full boil. Cook until the liquid thickens and starts to evaporate, about 4 minutes. Lower the heat and cook until the liquid evaporates further and the surface of the rice starts to become visible, another 5 minutes.

3 Stir in the coconut cream and continue to cook over low heat, stirring occasionally, until the rice grains are fully cooked, about 25 minutes. Remove from the heat and transfer to a deep dish. Smooth out the surface and set aside to cool. Refrigerate overnight before serving. To serve, dust the rice pudding with ground cinnamon.

Soaking the rice prior to cooking and using a heavy-bottomed pot are key elements in this recipe. Soaking it softens the grain and the thickness of the pot will prevent the milk products in the recipe from scorching.

Chapter VIII

Desserts

Tembleque

Coconut Pudding
Serves 10 to 12

Ingredients:

- 2 14-ounce cans Goya coconut milk
- 2¼ cups sugar
- ½ teaspoon salt
- 1 cup cornstarch
- Goya ground cinnamon for dusting

Procedure:

1 In a saucepan, combine the coconut milk with the sugar and salt. Bring to a full boil and cook for about 6 minutes, stirring occasionally. In a bowl, combine the cornstarch with ¾ cup of water and, with a whisk, mix well into a slurry. Immediately pour the slurry into the saucepan and cook, continuously whisking until the mixture thickens into a pudding, about 2 minutes. Remove from the heat.

2 Pour the mixture through a colander. Transfer the strained pudding into a nonstick 12"x6" deep dish or into individual martini glasses. Smooth out the surface, and set aside to cool. Refrigerate to completely set, about 2 hours. Dust the surface with ground cinnamon, slice, and serve.

Chapter VIII

Desserts

Pastelillos de Guayaba

Guava Pastries
Yields 12 pieces

Ingredients:

- 1 puff pastry sheet, about 12 ounces
- 1 pound guava paste
- confectioners' sugar for dusting

Procedure:

1 Preheat the oven to 350°F. Place the puff pastry sheet on a lightly floured flat surface. Cut into twelve 3"x3" squares and arrange on a baking sheet lined with parchment paper. Place in the oven and bake until the pastry puffs up, is lightly golden, and detaches itself easily from the parchment paper, about 10 minutes. Remove from the oven, and set aside to cool.

2 Meanwhile, place the guava paste in a food processor with ½ cup of water. Process to a smooth paste and transfer to a pastry bag with a small tip.

3 Insert the tip of the pastry bag into the center of a pastry square and fill with the guava mixture. Repeat with the remaining puff squares. Generously dust the guava pastries with confectioners' sugar. Serve with a glass of cold milk.

alcapurrias piononos pasteles
tostonera chillo rellenos de
alcapurrias piononos pasteles
tostonera chillo rellenos de papa pa
piononos pasteles arañitas tostones tosto
rellenos de papa pastelillos alc
pasteles arañitas tostones tostones
pastelillos alcapurrias piononos
tostones tostonera chillo rellenos
pastelillos alcapurrias piononos
tostones tostonera chillo rellenos
alcapurrias piononos pasteles

Step by Step

Watch Video at http://www.wilobenet.com/trueflavors

Pastelillos

Turnovers

1. On a cutting board or other flat surface place one *plantilla*.

2. Dip your fingers in the egg wash.

3. Lightly spread the egg wash on the edges of the *plantilla*.

4. Place the desired stuffing (in this case beef *picadillo*) in the center of the *plantilla*.

5. Fold over one half of the *plantilla* over the other to form a half moon shape and tuck the dough to make sure the edges are formed.

6. Lightly press with a fork to seal the edges

7. This is what the finished *pastelillo* should look like before frying.

8. Fry in 350°F oil until golden brown and blistered, which is the absolute authentic look.

Watch Video at http://www.wilobenet.com/trueflavors

Alcapurrias

Stuffed *Yautía* Fritters

1

Add the masa to the mold. A slight overflow is correct.

2

With the tip of your index finger lightly oiled, form a small hole in the center of the *masa*. Do not go through to the bottom of the mold.

3

With the index finger lightly oiled in a circular motion enlarge the well previously formed.

4

A slight overflow of the *masa* as shown is correct.

5

Fill the wells with ground meat or your choice of stuffing.

6

With the backside of a tablespoon lightly oiled, start replacing the overflow of *masa* towards the inside of each *alcapurria*.

If necessary add a little more *masa* in an effort to insure every *alcapurria* is completely sealed to prevent excess oil from going inside them. Freeze for approximately two hours or more.

Once frozen, remove the *alcapurrias* from the flexmolds when ready for frying.

Drop each *alcapurria* carefully in the 350°F oil, making sure there is plenty of space between them.

Fry approximately 4-5 minutes until golden brown and fully cooked inside.

Remove from the oil, drain on paper towels and serve hot.

Watch Video at http://www.wilobenet.com/trueflavors

Piononos

Ripe Plantain and Beef Molds

1. Start by peeling the ripe plantain.

2. Slice the plantain in ⅛ - ¼ inch thick slices.

3. Place the pieces in the frying oil at 350°F.

4. Once the plantains are fried to a light golden brown, remove from oil and let drain on a paper towel.

5. With tip of your fingers lightly oil the inside walls of a standard souffle mold, about 4" in diameter.

6. Cut out a round piece of parchment paper that fits snuggly in the bottom of the mold without the edges coming up on the sides. In other words, it should be equal or slightly smaller than the actual bottom of the mold.

Place the cut parchment on the bottom of the mold that has been previously greased.

Start placing the plantains in a orderly fashion to cover the bottom of the mold with the ripe plantain slices.

Cut one of the slices in four pieces to form triangles and use them to fill the still uncovered spaces and continue until completely covered.

Now start covering the sides without overlapping the slices but tucking them tight. It is important that the entire diameter is covered.

Fill the well with *picadillo* or your stuffing of preference, just to the edge as shown and the stuffing should be loose.

Pour whipped egg over the stuffing and help spread the egg throughout by stirring the stuffing gently.

You should end up with a thin layer of egg on top. Bake at 350°F for approximately 20-25 minutes. Once baked, remove from the oven and let rest for approximately 10 minutes.

Run a paring knife along the edges to help remove the *Pionono* from the mold and present it egg-side down.

225

Watch Video at http://www.wilobenet.com/trueflavors

Pasteles

Yautía and Pork "*Pasteles*"

1

Carefully place a plantain leaf over an open flame or other source of heat, being careful not to burn yourself and moving it back and forth somewhat rapidly.

2

Continue until the leaf turns a little shiny, which is when the leaf turns to a more pliable state so it can later be folded without cracking.

3

Pour the filling into the *masa*.

4

Stir and mix so all the ingredients are evenly distributed.

5

Make a heaping tablespoon of the *masa*.

6

Place the heaping tablespoon of the *masa* on the center of the plantain leaf.

Make a fold like when folding a letter.

Press gently from both ends inwards until the your fingers feel that it is taut, but not bursting.

Now tighten from the top as well.

Give it one last fold and retighten from the sides inward, as before.

Fold one side at a time inwards towards the center.

Repeat from the remaining side.

The *pastel* must remain with its folded side facing down so it doesn't open.

Watch Video at http://www.wilobenet.com/trueflavors

Arañitas

Plantain "Spiders"

1

To peel the green plantains first remove both ends with a pairing knife.

2

Score the plantains lengthwise about three to five times only skin deep.

3

From this point onward use surgical gloves to prevent staining your hands. Using the pairing knife, remove the tip of the first strip of skin by lightly lifting its corner.

4

Slide a finger under the corner of the skin that you just lifted and run your finger through until it is removed. This procedure is eased by using surgical gloves and doing it under running cold water.

5

Repeat this procedure until the plantain has been completely freed of its skin.

6

Once the plantains are peeled, grate them through the coarse side of a standard grater.

7

Do not place the grated plantains in water since this will wash off some of the necessary starch required to achieve this recipe.

8

Gently grab a small bunch with the tips of your fingers.

9

Form bundles without pressing them too much so they are just held together loosely.

10

Repeat until all the gratings have been shaped into small bundles, as shown.

11

Carefully drop the bundles one at a time into the hot oil 350°F.

12

Place the *arañitas* in the oil, making sure they don't touch each other, to prevent them from sticking together.

13

Fry for approximately 8-10 minutes.

14

Carefully remove from the oil and place the *arañitas* on a piece of paper towel to rid them of excess oil. Sprinkle with salt while hot and serve.

Watch Video at http://www.wilobenet.com/trueflavors

Tostones Tradicionales

Plantain *"Tostones"*

1

To peel the green plantains, first remove both ends with a pairing knife.

2

Score the plantains lengthwise about three to five times only skin deep.

3

From this point onward use surgical gloves to prevent staining your hands. Using the pairing knife, remove the tip of the first strip of skin by lightly lifting its corner.

4

Slide a finger under the corner of the skin that you just lifted and run your finger through until it is removed. This procedure is eased by using surgical gloves and doing it under running cold water.

5

Repeat this procedure until the plantain has been completely freed of its skin.

6

Cut the plantain in one-inch pieces.

Place the pieces in the frying oil at 350°F.

While the plantains are frying, lightly oil the back of a small pan and set aside.

Remember you don't have to fully cook the plantains at this stage. Remove the plantains from the frying pan once they are light golden brown in color and still somewhat raw inside.

Place one plantain piece under the lightly oiled bottom of the pan as shown and press to flatten. The flatter you can make them, the crispier they will be in the end.

Slide a pairing knife under the flattened *Tostón* to help detach it from the pan.

Fry the flattened plantains, now *Tostones*, until crisp. Drain on paper towels and serve hot.

Watch Video at http://www.wilobenet.com/trueflavors

Tostones con Tostonera
Plantain *"Tostones"* with *Tostonera*

To peel the green plantains, first remove both ends with a pairing knife.

Score the plantains lengthwise about three to five times only skin deep.

From this point onward, use surgical gloves to prevent staining your hands. Using the pairing knife, remove the tip of the first strip of skin by lightly lifting its corner.

Slide a finger under the corner of the skin that you just lifted and run your finger through until it is removed. This procedure is eased by using surgical gloves and doing it under running cold water.

Repeat this procedure until the plantain has been completely freed of its skin.

Cut the plantain in one-inch pieces.

These are two types of *tostoneras*: the thick one is for the stuffing kind and the thin one for the standard flat *tostón*.

Notice the slim cavity on the bottom of the standard *tostonera*.

Fry the inch-thick pieces of green plantain until golden brown and still raw in the inside.

Place the first fried plantain in the center of the slim cavity on the bottom end of the *tostonera*.

Fold the top part over the bottom, to sandwich the plantain in between.

Apply pressure to ensure the plantain is flattened as much as the *tostonera* will allow.

Open the *tostonera*,

Use a sharp knife to easily remove the *Tostón*.

The *Tostones* should be thin as shown.

Fry the flattened plantains, now *Tostones*, until crisp. Drain on paper towels and serve hot.

Watch Video at http://www.wilobenet.com/trueflavors

Tostones Rellenos

Plantain Stuffed *"Tostones"* with *Tostonera*

1

To peel the green plantains, first remove both ends with a pairing knife.

2

Score the plantains lengthwise about three to five times only skin deep.

3

From this point onward, use surgical gloves to prevent staining your hands. Using the pairing knife, remove the tip of the first strip of skin by lightly lifting its corner.

4

Slide a finger under the corner of the skin that you just lifted and run your finger through until it is removed. This procedure is eased by using surgical gloves and doing it under running cold water.

5

Repeat this procedure until the plantain has been completely freed of its skin.

6

Cut the plantain in one-inch pieces.

7

These are two types of *tostoneras*: The thick one is for the stuffing kind and the thin one for the standard flat *tostón*.

8

Notice the deep cavity on the bottom end of the standard *tostonera*.

9

Place the pieces in the frying oil at 350°F.

10

Place the first fried plantain in the center of the deep cavity on the bottom end of the *tostonera*.

11

Fold the top part over the bottom to sandwich the plantain in between.

12

Apply pressure to ensure the plantain is flattened as much as the *tostonera* will allow.

13

Open the *tostonera*.

14

Carefully remove the *tostón* from the *tostonera* by excercising light rotation while you hold the *tostón* by the tip of your fingers.

15

The tostón should come out in one piece, as shown,

16

Place the pieces in the frying oil at 350°F and fry until crisp. Drain on paper towels and serve hot.

Watch Video at http://www.wilobenet.com/trueflavors

Chillo Frito
Fried Red Snapper

1. Start with a fresh Red Snapper approximately 1½-2 pounds in weight. The fish should be gutted, scaled and fully dressed.

2. Make diagonal incisions bone deep on the fillet, guiding yourself with the angle in which the gills are placed to establish uniformity, keeping incisions an inch apart.

3. Now score the same fillet diagonally using the same distance you used for the first diagonal incisions, to create squares/diamonds out of the fillet.

4. Repeat the process until the entire side has been scored, as shown, all the way to the tail's end.

5. Repeat for the other side of the fish keeping all the same parameters in an effort to insure uniformity.

6. Score until you reach the end of the tail.

7

This shows exactly how the fish should look after it has been scored.

8

Sprinkle with *adobo* generously on both sides, making sure the incisions get some of the *adobo*.

9

Dredge with all purpose flour or cornstarch on both sides.

10

Dredge with all purpose flour or cornstarch on both sides.

11

Shake off any excess flour by gently shaking the fish as shown.

12

Bend the fish in a way that mouth and tail somewhat touch each other and place a wooden skewer through the fish to preserve the bent shape. At this point the fish should stand on its own.

13

Add another skewer to insure the fish will not unfold in the frying process later.

14

Hold the fish carefully by its dorsal fin, and drop the fish in oil at 350°F.

15

Notice the size of the pot selected for this procedure. This pot is considerably larger than the one required, to allow for the oil overflow that will be created by the fish and residual moisture when it is dropped into the oil.

16

Using a pair of metal kitchen tongs carefully remove the fish from the frying oil and drain on paper towels. Serve with Creole Sauce. (See recipe on page 12)

Watch Video at http://www.wilobenet.com/trueflavors

Rellenos de Papa

Stuffed Potato Fritters

1

Dip the scoop in water and shake to remove excess water.

2

Fill the scoop and press against the sides of the bowl to insure it is packed tightly.

3

With your index finger lightly dipped in oil, press the center to form a cavity.

4

Work your finger delicately in a circular motion to carefully expand the well.

5

At this point the overflow shown is what we are looking for, since after stuffing the overflow will help us close the dumpling.

6

Fill the well with ground meat making sure to leave space for the cheese.

Add a small cube of cream cheese.

Press the cheese and tuck in well, making sure the top of the cheese leaves clearing for the closing stage.

Carefully and with short strokes empty the dumpling into the palm of your hand.

Start folding the potato overflow from the outside towards the inside, to close the dumpling, making sure there are no exposed particles of meat.

Once the dumpling is closed, gently roll in the palm of your hand.

Continue rolling until the dumpling is clearly round and free of lumps.

Roll in cornstarch.

Remove excess cornstarch.

Carefully drop in the 350°F frying oil.

Continue frying until golden brown.

Remove carefully from the oil, drain on paper towels and serve hot.

Glossary

adobo (ah-DO-bo):
Puerto Rico's staple seasoning composed mainly of garlic and oregano. Fresh and dried versions of the seasoning can be easily concocted.

achiote (ah-chee-O-tay):
Also known as "*annatto*"; the small seed of the fruit from a small native West Indian tree. It is commonly used to give foods a red hue. Taíno indians used this seed to dye their skin.

achiote oil (ah-chee-O-tay oil):
Oil made out of steeping *achiote* seeds (see *achiote*) in vegetable oil. It is used as a coloring base for stews and rice dishes.

ají dulce (ah-HEE DUL-say):
Meaning "sweet pepper"; a small, pudgy pepper, similar in shape to the Scotch Bonnet. It ranges in color from green to orange and red and is an important ingredient in *sofrito*.

ají caballero (ah-HEE cah-bah-YAY-ro):
A small pointy chili pepper ranging from green to orange or red. It is the main ingredient in Puerto Rican homemade hot sauce (see *pique*). It is probably called *caballero* (gentleman) because it grows upright in the bush.

alcaparrado: (Al-cah-pah-RAH-do):
A Spanish mixture of capers, olives and peppers.

alcaparras: (Al-cah-pah-RAHS):
Spanish word for "capers".

amarillos (ah-ma-REE-yos):
Spanish for "yellow". Term used to refer to fried ripe plantains.

apio (AH-pee-o):
Edible root of a tropical plant. It has a bright yellow flesh with a sweet and bread-like taste. Not to be confused with "celery", also referred to as *apio*.

arroz (ah-ROSS):
Spanish word for "rice". In Puerto Rico, short and medium grain is the norm.

asopao (ah-so-POW):
A soupy rice dish made traditionally with chicken. It is also made with shrimp, or with pigeon peas.

bacalao (bah-cah-LAH-o):
Cod fish that has been salted and air-dried. It is very common throughout the island. Once a cheap product, *bacalao* has become increasingly expensive with time.

baño de maria (ban-yo day maria):
(baine de marie, F.) A method of oven cooking: put the pan with the ingredients into a larger pan containing water. The water should not reach more than 3/4 up the sides of the smaller pan.

breadfruit:
Believed to be introduced to the West Indies by Captain Bligh of the Bounty, it is a large fruit containing pulp that is cooked as a vegetable. Also see *pana*.

calabaza (ka-lah-BAH-zah):
West Indian pumpkin with a freckled skin and orange flesh. It is mashed to make soups and fritters or cut and added to stews as a thickening agent.

caldero (cal-DAY-ro):
Meaning "cauldron"; made of aluminum, it is the cooking vessel of choice in Puerto Rican homes, particularly for cooking rice.

caribbean pumpkin:
see *calabaza*

carrucho (ca-ROO-cho):
Spanish word for "conch"; a Caribbean mollusk that lives mostly inside large conch shells. Its meat is similar in taste and texture to that of clams.

chayote: (Chi-YO-tay):
A popular island squash, round or pear-shaped, which can be eaten raw or cooked.

chillo (CHIL-lyo):
"Red Snapper". It is the most common fish consumed throughout the island, served mostly whole, breaded and fried.

chuletas (choo-LAY-tah):
Puerto Rican term for "pork chops" or "chops".

coconut milk:
Made by combining equal parts water and shredded fresh coconut. Simmer until foamy; strain, and squeeze out the liquid.

coconut cream:
Made by combining 1 parts water and 4 parts coconut meat and simmering until foamy. Mixture is then strained, squeezing much of the liquid.

---

colmadito (Col-MAH-De-toe):
Small (usually neighborhood) grocery store selling packaged as well as prepared foods.

cubanelle peppers:
Elongated sweet pepper, also called banana peppers, light green with spots of red and orange, with a more herbal taste than its cousin, the Bell pepper.

culantro (coo-LAHN-tro):
also known as "long leaf *cilantro*". Another important element in *sofrito*, it grows easily and rapidly in households throughout the island.

empanada (em-pah-NAH-dah):
referring to a piece of meat (pork, chicken, beef or fish and seafood) that has been breaded and fried.

fonda: (Fon-DAH)
A small, casual restaurant.

fortified wine:
Those wines which have had their alcoholic content increased during production, resulting in the retaining of its natural sugar. Includes port, sherry and Madeira.

funche (FOON-chay):
The Puerto Rican equivalent to polenta or grits. It is a creamy preparation of cornmeal. Proteins such as salt cod or sardines are incorporated into the cornmeal for a hearty one-pot meal.

---

gandules (gan-DOO-lays):
Spanish for "pigeon peas".

green banana:
An eating banana that has not yet ripened to a yellow-skin state; usually boiled for "*guineitos*" or prepared as "*guineitos en escabeche*".

grosellas: (Gro-SAY-as):
A currant; Grosellas *Silvestres* is a gooseberry.

jamonilla (hah-mo-NEE-yah):
Spanish for "luncheon meat". Surprisingly, there is a strong "luncheon meat" culture in Puerto Rico, which is used in preparations from sandwich spreads to rice and stews.

mojo (MO-ho):
In Puerto Rico, a *mojo* is a sauce usually containing a tomato product, but garlic and oil *mojos* are also served over fried plantains or boiled root vegetables. The word "*mojo*" probably derives from the term *mojar* which means "to wet".

mofongo (moh-FON-goh):
Staple island dish made with green plantains that are fried and mashed with garlic and pork cracklings in a *pilón*.

ñame (NYAH-may):
Root vegetable with a bark-like skin and a white starchy flesh. Compared to other tubers, its taste is slightly bitter.

jueyes (hoo-AY-es):
Puerto Rican "land crabs". Their meat is darker than that of blue crabs, and sweeter due to their corn-based diet.

longaniza (lon-gah-NEE-zah):
Spanish pork sausage seasoned with paprika, cinnamon, anise seed, garlic and vinegar.

olive oil:
Olive oil is the product extracted from a single vegetable; olives. It is easily digested and has a fruity taste.

---

pana: (pah-nah):
Puerto Rican term for "bread fruit", also called *panapen*; the green fruit of a tropical tree. It has a starchy white pulp that can be prepared the same way as a potato, baked, boiled, fried or roasted.

pasteles (pas-TAY-lays):
The Puerto Rican version of Mexican *tamales* or Venezuelan *ayacas*. Traditionally, a *masa* of green bananas is stuffed with pork and other condiments, wrapped in a plantain leaf and boiled. *Yautía* and *yuca* are often used to prepare the *masa*.

Glossary

pastelillo (pahs-tay-LEE-yo):
Puerto Rican term for "turnover" or what is commonly known throughout Latin America and the Caribbean as an *empanada*.

picadillo (pee-cah-DEE-yo):
Name given to ground beef that is cooked with *sofrito* and other condiments. It is consumed on its own, or used as stuffing in many typical recipes.

plantain: (Plan-TANE):
A tropical cooking banana, larger than an eating banana, used in a myriad of recipes.

plantilla (plan-TEE-yah):
Ready-made dough rounds made with flour and tinted with *achiote* oil; they are stuffed and fried to make *pastelillos*.

pilón (pee-LON):
Traditional mortar and pestle. It is made out of wood and is used on an everyday basis to pound garlic down to a paste.

pique (PEE-kay):
Puerto Rican homemade vinegar-based hot sauce made with *ají caballero*, garlic and *culantro*. Traditionally stored and sold in a *caneca*, a small recycled rum bottle.

queso fresco del país (kay-so FRES-co dehl pah-EES):
Puerto Rican farmer's-style white cheese with a bland taste and a bouncy, grainy texture. It is great for frying or for complementing sweet or salty foods.

racimo: (Ra-see-MO):
A large stalk of plantains or bananas.

revoltillo : (Rev-ole-ta-YO):
Meaning "turned around, scrambled", as in scrambled eggs.

ripe plantains:
These are the plantains that have ripened to a skin-color ranging from yellow, to yellow with dark spots, to heavily spotted, almost black skins.

sofrito (SOH-FREE-to):
A seasoning consisting of onion, garlic, peppers and *culantro*, used as a base in most Puerto Rican dishes.

Spanish tomato sauce:

Traditional Spanish-style canned tomato sauce made with tomatoes, peppers and spices. The Goya brand is available in any supermarket.

tallarines : (Tah-yar-INES):
Small bundles of dried, thin noodles, used in Chicken Noodle Soup.

tocino (toh-SEE-no):
Meaning "salt pork"; it is often used to flavor the oil for stewed beans and other preparations.

tostones (tos-TOH-nays):
Term used to refer to a smashed piece of fried green plantain or any other fried starchy root vegetable. The traditional way to smash the vegetables is a *tostonera*, two wooden planks clipped together with a metal rod.

volao (VO-LAUW):
Fried to the point of perfection, being both crisp and light.

yautía (yah-oo-TEE-ah):
Also known as *malanga* (ma-LAHN-gah); a shaggy-textured tuber commonly used in Puerto Rican cuisine. In its ground state it is used as *masa* for different typical preparations such as *alcapurrias* and *pasteles*.
There is a variety of *yautía* called *yautía lila* because of its purplish color.

yuca (YOO-kah):
Also known as cassava or manioc, it is a starchy edible root with a bark-like skin and a fibrous and milky texture. It is cooked and eaten like yams or potatoes.

 ACHIOTE

 AJI CABALLERO

 AJI DULCE

 ALCAPARRADO

 AMERICAN CHAYOTE

 APIO

 AVOCADO

 BAY LEAF

PICTURED BASICS

 CILANTRO

 COCONUT

 CUBANELLE PEPPERS

 FARMER'S CHEESE

 GANDULES

 GARLIC MOJITO

 GREEN BANANAS

 GREEN PLANTAINS

 GUAVA PASTE

 GUAYABAS / GUAVAS

 GUINGAMBO / OKRA

 LIMES

 LOCAL CHAYOTE

 ESCABECHE

 ÑAME

 OREGANO

 PAPAYA

 PINK BEANS

 PLANTAIN LEAVES

 MOJITO ISLEÑO

 ACHIOTE OIL

 CARIBBEAN PUMPKIN

 RECAO / CULANTRO

 RED BEANS

 RIPLE PLANTAINS

 SALT COD

 SPANISH TOMATO SAUCE

 SWEET POTATO

 TANIER / YAUTIA

 WHITE BEANS

 YUCA / CASSAVA

pique sofrito mojito achiote a
che mayoketchup pique sofrito
mójili adobo escabeche ma
jito achiote ajili mójili adobo
pique sofrito mojito achiote
beche mayoketchup pique sof
li mójili adobo escabeche may
o mojito achiote ajili mójili
ayoketchup pique sofrito mojit
o escabeche mayoketchup pi
hiote ajili mójili adobo esca
pique sofrito mojito achiote a

Index

Adobo
Dry Rub 6

Alcapurrias
Stuffed *Yautía* Fritters 41
Step by Step 222

Ají
caballeros 7, 11
dulce 7, 13, 37

Apio
Mashed Root Vegetables (*Viandas Majadas*) 61

B

Beans
Chickpeas with Chorizo, Stewed (*Garbanzos Guisados con Chorizo*) 129
and Pig's Feet Stew (*Patitas de Cerdo con Garbanzos*) 103
Pigeon Peas with Plaintain Dumplings (*Gandules con Bolitas de Plátano*) 127
Red Kidney, Stewed (*Habichuelas Rojas Guisadas*) 133
Rice with Chickpeas and Chorizo (*Arroz con Garbanzos y Chorizo*) 114
White, Stewed (*Habichuelas Blancas Guisadas*) 131

Beef
and Plantain Lasagna (*Piñon*) 65
Breaded, Cutlets (*Bistec Empanado*) 157
Breaded, Cutlets, Parmesan (*Empanada Parmesana*) 159
Corned 91
Lasagna, Puerto Rican Style (*Lasaña Criolla*) 139
Pot Roast, Stuffed (*Carne Mechada*) 175
Steak with Onions (*Bistec Encebollado*) 162
Ripe Plantain and Beef Lasagna (*Piñon*) 65
Ripe Plantain and Beef Rolls (*Pinononos*) 67
and Root Vegetable Stew (*Sancocho*) 95
Salted Beef Stew (*Tasajo*) 105
Skirt Steak (*Churrasco*) 161
Spiced Ground, (*Picadillo*) 167
Steaks with Onions (*Bistec Encebollado*) 162
Stew (*Carne Guisada*) 101

Breadfruit
"Tostones" (*Tostones de Pana*) 49

Candy
Candied Papaya (*Dulce de Lechosa*) 205

Cheese
Fried Cheese Balls (*Bolitas de Queso*) 33
Fritters, (*Almojábanas*) 39
Fried Cheese (*Queso Frito del País*) 19
and Guava Turnovers (*Pastelillos de Guayaba*) 23
Stuffed (*Queso Relleno*) 171
Turnovers (*Pastelillos de Queso*) 21

Chayote
American 169

Chicken
Cracklings, Fried (*Chicharrones de Pollo*) 27
Fried (*Pollo Frito*) 149
Noodle Soup, (*Sopa de Pollo y Fideos*) 77
with Rice (*con Arroz*) 111
Roast (*Pollo al Horno*) 147
Spaghetti with, *Criollo*-style (*Espagueti con Pollo Criollo*) 137
Stew (*Fricasé de Pollo*) 97
Stock (*Caldo de Pollo*) 72
Whole, method of cutting (*Pollo al Horno*) 147

Chips
Plantain Chips (*Platanutres*) 45

Cod Fish
Baked, with Potatoes (*Bacalao a la Vizcaína*) 193
Fried (*Bacalaitos*) 35
Salad with Root Vegetables (*Serenata de Bacalao*) 190
Salt Cod Cakes (*Buñuelos de Bacalao*) 36
Salt Cod Polenta (*Funche con Bacalao*) 195
and Scrambled Eggs (*Revoltillo con Bacalao*) 197
with Stewed Eggplant (*Berenjena Guisada con Bacalao*) 87

Condiments, prepared
Sofrito 13
Ajili mójili 7
Escabeche 8
Mayoketchup 9
Mojito 10
Mojo Isleño 12
Pique 11
Salsa Criolla 12

Cornmeal
Salt-Cod Polenta (*Funche con Bacalao*) 195
Salty Fried Corn Stick Fritters (*Sorullos/Saladitos*) 29
Sweet Fried Corn Stick Fritters (*Sorullos Dulces*) 31

Crab Meat
Rice with Crabmeat (*Arroz con Jueyes*) 117
Crabmeat "Salmorejo" (*Salmorejo de Jueyes*) 189

Custards
Cheese (*Flan de Queso*) 207
Coconut (*Flan de Coco*) 208
Vanilla (*Flan de Vainilla*) 209

Dips
Ajili mójili 7
Mayoketchup 9

Dressings
Mayoketchup 9
Mojito 10

Fish (also see Cod and Shellfish)
Conch Salad (*Ensalada de Carrucho*) 180
Kingfish, Pickled (*Sierra en Escabeche*) 199
Octopus Salad (*Ensalada de Pulpo*) 182
Red Snapper, Fried (*Chillo Frito*) 201
Stock (*Caldo de Pescado*) 75

Goat
Stewed Goat (*Fricasé de Cabrito*) 99

Meat (also see Beef and Pork)
Rice with Luncheon Meat (*Arroz con Jamonilla*) 115
Luncheon Meat Sandwiches (*Sándwiches de Mezcla*) 143
Meat Sauce with Criollo-style Spaghetti (*Espagueti con Carne Criolla*) 135
Stewed Luncheon Meat (*Jamonilla Guisada*) 93
Stock (*Caldo de Res*) 73
Turnovers (*Pastelillos de Carne*) 24

Mofongo
Cassava (*de Yuca*) 59
Green Plantain (*de Plátano*) 57
Ripe Plantain (*de Amarillo*) 55

Mojito
Garlic 10
with *Yuca* 10

Mortar and Pestle
Cassava (*de Yuca*) 59
Green Plantain (*de Plátano*) 57

Noodles
with Chicken Soup (*Sopa de Pollo y Fideos*) 77
Lasagana, Puerto Rican Style (*Lasaña Criolla*) 139
Spaghetti, Criollo Style with Meat Sauce (*Espagueti con Carne Criolla*) 135
Spaghetti, Criollo Style with Chicken (*Espagueti con Pollo Criollo*) 137

Oils
Annato (*Aceite de Achiote*) 6

Papaya
Candied (*Dulce de Lechosa*) 205

Pasteles
Yautía and Pork Dumplings (*Pasteles*) 68
Step by Step 226

Pastries
Guava (*Pastelillos de Guayaba*) 23

Pickling
About (*Escabeche*) 8
Escabeche 8
Kingfish (*Sierra en Escabeche*) 199

Plantains
About
Chips (*Platanutres*) 45
Dumplings, with Pigeon Peas (*Gandules con Bolitas de Plátano*) 127
Green "Mofongo" (*Mofongo de Plátano*) 57
Plantain Soup (*Sopa de Plátano*) 83
Ripe "*Mofongo*" (*Mofongo de Amarillo*) 55
Ripe Plantain and Beef Lasagna (*Piñón*) 65
Ripe Plantain and Beef Mold (*Piononos*) 67
"Spiders" (*Arañitas*) 51
Sweet, in Syrup (*Amarillos en Almíbar*) 53

Plantilla Rounds
Cheese Turnovers (*Pastelillos de Queso*) 21
Guava and Chesse Turnovers (*Pastelillos de Guayaba*) 23
Meat Turnovers (*Pastelillos de Carne*) 24
Step by Step 220

Pork
Chickpea and Pig's Feet Stew (*Patitas de Cerdo con Garbanzos*) 103
Fried (*Carne Frita*) 165
Fried Chops (*Chuletas Fritas*) 153
Ham with Pineapple Sauce (*Jamón con Piña*) 172
Criollo Pork Sausage (*Longaniza*) 145
Roast Pork Butt (*Pernil*) 155

Potatoes
Salad (*Ensalada de Papa*) 63
Stuffed Potato Fritters (*Rellenos de Papa*) 40

Puddings
Bread (*Budín de Pan*) 211
Rice (*Arroz con Dulce*) 213
Coconut (*Tembleque*) 215

Pumpkin
Fried (*Frituras de Calabaza; Barrigas de Vieja*) 25
Puree 25
Soup (*Sopa de Calabaza*) 85

Rice
Arroz Pegao 16
and Chicken Soup (*Asopao de Pollo*) 79
Stuffed (*Relleno*) 125
White (*Blanco*) 111
with Chicken (*con Pollo*) 121
with Chickpeas and Chorizo (*con Garbanzos y Chorizo*) 114
with Crabmeat (*con Jueyes*) 117
with Luncheon Meat (*con Jamonilla*) 115
with Loganiza Sausage 119
with Chicken (*con pollo*) 121
with Corn (*con Maíz*) 116
with Pigeon Peas (*con Gandules*) 113
Pudding (*con Dulce*) 213
with Vienna Sausages (*con Salchichas*) 123

Rubs
Adobo 6

249

Salads
Conch (*Ensalada de Carrucho*) 180
Octopus (*Ensalada de Pulpo*) 182
Potato (*Ensalada de Papa*) 63
Root Vegetable Salad with Salt Cod (*Serenata de Bacalao*) 190

Sauces
Ajili mójili 7
Garlic Sauce, Shrimp in (*Camarones al Ajillo*) 185
Mojo Isleño 12
Pineapple Sauce, with Ham (*Jamón con Piña*) 172
Salsa Criolla 12
Sofrito 13

Sausage
Chorizo, Stewed Chickpeas with (*Garbanzos con Chorizo*) 129
Criollo Pork Sausage (*Longaniza*) 145
Longaniza with Rice (*Arroz con Longaniza*) 119
Rice with Chickpeas and Chorizo (*Arroz con Garbanzos y Chorizo*) 114
Rice with Vienna Sausage (*Arroz con Salchichas*) 123

Shellfish
Conch Salad (*Ensalada de Carrucho*) 180
Crabmeat "*Salmorejo*" (*Salmorejo de Jueyes*) 189
Rice with Crab Meat (*Arroz con Jueyes*) 117
Lobster with Garlic Sauce (*Langosta al Ajillo*) 187
Shrimp in Garlic Sauce (*Camarones al Ajillo*) 185

Soups
Chicken Noodle (*Sopa de Pollo y Fideos*) 77
Chicken and Rice (*Asopao de Pollo*) 78
Caribbean Pumpkin Soup (*Sopa de Calabaza*) 85
Plantain Soup (*Sopa de Plátano*) 83
Root Vegetable Soup (*Sopa de Viandas*) 81

Step by Step
Turnovers (*Pastelillos*) 220
Stuffed *Yautía* Fritters (*Alcapurrias*) 222
Ripe Plantain and Beef Mold (*Piononos*) 224
Yautía and Pork Dumplings (*Pasteles*) 226
Plantain "Spiders" (*Arañitas*) 228
Plantain "*Tostones*" (*Tostones Tradicionales*) 230
Plantain "*Tostones*" with *Tostonera* (*Tostones con Tostonera*) 232
Plantain Stuffed "*Tostones*" with *Tostonera* (*Tostones Rellenos*) 234
Fried Red Snapper (*Chillo Frito*) 236
Stuffed Potato Fritters (*Rellenos de Papa*) 238

Stews
Baked Salt Cod Stew with Potatoes (*Bacalao a la Vizcaína*) 193
Beef (*Carne Guisada*) 101
Chicken (*Fricasé de Pollo*) 97
Salted Beef (*Tasajo*) 105
Chickpea and Pig's Feet (*Patitas de Cerdo con Garbanzos*) 103
Eggplant (*Berenjena Guisada*) 87
Goat (*Fricasé de Cabrito*) 99
Luncheon Meat (*Jamonilla Guisada*) 93
Okra (*Guingambó Guisado*) 89
Red Kidney Beans (*Habichuelas Rojas Guisadas*) 133
Salt Cod and Eggplant (*Berenjena Guisada con Bacalao*) 87
Veal (*Fricasé de Ternera*) 98
White Beans (*Habichuelas Blancas Guisadas*) 131

Stocks
Beef (*Caldo de Res*) 73
Chicken (*Caldo de Pollo*) 72
Fish (*Caldo de Pescado*) 75

Tostones
Green Plantain (de Plátano) 47
Breadfruit (de Pana) 49
Step by Step 230, 232, 234

Turkey
Roasted, Puerto Rican-style (*Pavo Criollo al Horno*) 151

Vegetables
Chayotes, Stuffed (*Chayotes Rellenos*) 168
Rice with Corn (*Arroz con Maíz*) 116
Eggplant, Stewed (*Berenjena Guisada*) 87
Mashed Root (*Viandas Majadas*) 61
Okra (*Guingambó*) 89
Potatoes in Baked Salt Cod (*Bacalao a la Vizcaína*) 193
Root Vegetable & Beef Stew (*Sancocho*) 95
Root Vegetable Salad with Salt Cod (*Serenata de Bacalao*) 190
Root Vegetable Soup (*Sopa de Vivandas*) 81

Yautía
and Pork Dumplings (*Pasteles*) 68
Stuffed *Yautía* Fritters (*Alcapurrias*) 41

Yuca
Mofongo 59
Pickled (*Escabeche*) 199